TECHNOLOGY DEVELOPMENT AND MARKETING

With Cases & Theories

Junmo Kim
Konkuk University, Seoul, Korea

authorHOUSE®

AuthorHouse™
1663 Liberty Drive
Bloomington, IN 47403
www.authorhouse.com
Phone: 1 (800) 839-8640

© 2018 Junmo Kim. All rights reserved.

No part of this book may be reproduced, stored in a retrieval system, or transmitted by any means without the written permission of the author.

Published by AuthorHouse 06/06/2018

ISBN: 978-1-5462-4577-3 (sc)
ISBN: 978-1-5462-4576-6 (e)

Print information available on the last page.

Any people depicted in stock imagery provided by Getty Images are models, and such images are being used for illustrative purposes only.
Certain stock imagery © Getty Images.

This book is printed on acid-free paper.

Because of the dynamic nature of the Internet, any web addresses or links contained in this book may have changed since publication and may no longer be valid. The views expressed in this work are solely those of the author and do not necessarily reflect the views of the publisher, and the publisher hereby disclaims any responsibility for them.

CONTENTS

List of Figures ix
List of Tables xi
Preface xv

Chapter 1 Theories of Technology Marketing 1
Chapter 2 Trends of IT technology Development 16
Chapter 3 Evaluation on Technology Marketing 39
Chapter 4 Technology Trend and the World Market 69
Chapter 5 Failure cases of marketing: implications for technology
              development 75
Chapter 6 Conclusion 84

Appendix 87
Bibliography 95
Index 109

To my Lord, Jesus Christ

LIST OF FIGURES

Figure 1-1 Technology Life Cycle 1
Figure 1-2 BCG Matrix 6
Figure 1-3 Technology Cycles in Summary 7
Figure 2-1 Annual Growth of Electronics Market 16
Figure 2-2 Trend of heat pressure packaging 17
Figure 2-3 Trend of Conductive Adhesive packaging 18
Figure 2-4 FPCB Market forecast: quantity & sales volume 35
Figure 2-5 FPCB Market Forecast: quantity & Average price 35
Figure 2-6 Plotting of FPCB Market forecast: quantity & sales volume 36
Figure 2-7 Proportion of camera equipped cell phones among total cell phones market 37
Figure 2-8 Numbers of camera equipped cell phones by country ... 38
Figure 3-1 Technology side ordering from survey 67
Figure 3-2 Positioning of the four types 68
Figure 4-1 Broadband convergence network 69
Figure 4-2 Mobile phone subscribers per 100 inhabitants 1997-2007 71

LIST OF TABLES

Table 1-1 Characteristics by stages of Technology life Cycle............ 3
Table 1-2 Technology Development Cooperation stages................. 9
Table 1-3 Time Gap between the leader and followers 11
Table 1-4 Sectors of innovation origin and users of innovation (1945~83).. 12
Table 1-5 Major milestones of semiconductor industry of Korea 14
Table 1-6 Generational division of cell phones 15
Table 2-1 Forecast of packaging ratio 25
Table 2-2 Forecast of Bare chip use.. 27
Table 2-3 Requirements for SOC/SIP 27
Table 2-4 Forecast for Chip dimension requirements unit: mm 28
Table 2-5 Trends in Environmental Adpatation 30
Table 2-6 Technology Requirements for wireless devices 32
Table 2-7 Electronics packaging market: cell phone case 32
Table 2-8 Electronics packaging market size for Flat Display Panels 33
Table 2-9 Economic Impacts of micro packaging technology......... 33
Table 2-10 FPCB Market Forecast 34
Table 2-11 Economic Impacts of micro packaging material............ 36
Table 3-1 Positioning on R& D stage... 41
Table 3-2 Degrees of innovativeness in technology development project 42
Table 3-3 Diagnosis of technology: congruence with the technology trend in relevant technology clusters...................... 43
Table 3-4 Relative positioning on technology life cycle curve 44
Table 3-5 Easiness to protect patent rights of technology under development 45
Table 3-6 Application to markets... 46
Table 3-7 Existence of potential markets and the coverage of Industrial linkages... 47
Table 3-8 Positioning of Related markets and industries on Technology life Cycles.. 48

Table 3-9 Magnitude of market demands for patented technology of the field 49
Table 3-10 Entry Barriers due to regulation policy or other institutions 50
Table 3-11 Outside View: Positioning on R&D stage 51
Table 3-12 Outside View: Degrees of innovativeness in technology development project 52
Table 3-13 Outside View: Diagnosis of technology: congruence with the technology trend in relevant technology clusters 53
Table 3-14 Outside View: Relative positioning on technology life cycle curve 54
Table 3-15 Outside View: Easiness to protect patent rights of technology under development 55
Table 3-16 Outside View: Application to markets 56
Table 3-17 Outside View: Existence of potential markets and the coverage of Industrial linkages 57
Table 3-18 Outside View: Positioning of Related markets and industries on Technology life Cycles 58
Table 3-19 Outside View: Magnitude of market demands for patented technology of the field 59
Table 3-20 Time gap (% of responses by outside evaluators) 60
Table 3-21 Design competitiveness (row %) 61
Table 3-22 Performance competitiveness 62
Table 3-23 Brand Image 62
Table 3-24 Pricing policy comparison 63
Table 3-25 Expected Customer service competitiveness 63
Table 3-26 Expected Advertising competitiveness 64
Table 3-27 Expected distribution network competitiveness 65
Table 3-28 Expected profitability comparison 65
Table 3-29 Summery of time gap 66
Table 3-30 Market potential vs. technical completeness 67
Table 4-1 Generational division of Mobile phone market 70
Table 4-2 World electronics products & technology market size 72
Table 4-3 Forecast for major digital products 72
Table 4-4 Forecast for semiconductor application market 73

Table 4-5 Relative proportion among products 73
Table 4-6 Worldwide semiconductor market for automobiles 73
Table 4-7 Worldwide semiconductor equipment and material
    market growth 74
Table 4-8 Worldwide semiconductor packaging equipment
    market trend 74

PREFACE

Technology development needs a market. Since technology development is from supply side, it is always crucial to pay attention to demand side of technology. Taking this notion as an underling assumption, this book discussed a technology development case in the realm of micro electronic packaging technology based on a real case study of a three year consecutive R&D program conducted in Korea.

Through long years of technology development since the 20th century, we have been watching cases where seemingly superior technology fails to meet market demand. Sometimes technologies came out too early to be warmly received. Thus, technology development, from an innovator's point of view, should address potential demand submerged in society. In comparison, technology development, from a late comer's point of view, could be justified not only in technological viability to develop something within a given time frame, but also be convinced financially while meeting market demand and expectation.

The technology development case dealt in this book was a catch-up example, in which ample possibilities of market demand were expected. To elaborate a technology development case with a balance of theory and practice, chapter one of the book discussed theoretical contents including technology life cycle and technology adoption life cycles. Also a discussion was presented on an empirical study that implies lessons for technology life cycle in development.

Chapter two discussed trends of IT technology development in micro packaging. Chapter 3 paid attention on evaluation on Technology Marketing. In this evaluation, there was a two group evaluation for the four sub technology projects under micro packaging. Chapter 4 Technology Trend and the World Market tried to present technology trend for products within a broader range of consumer electronics product. Chapter 5 touched on failure cases in which individual technologies themselves were viable.

The publication of this book was made possible with my sabbatical research year spent in Austin Texas as well as the following period in Seoul after the sabbatical year. I would like to express my gratitude to faculty and staff members who have given various support. Though not mentioned, I believe that there are many other significant persons who have given positive encouragements to my life and research.

CHAPTER 1

THEORIES OF TECHNOLOGY MARKETING

1. Technology Life Cycle/ Product Life Cycle Theory

Since Vernon's pioneering work to introduce product life cycle theory, the theory of product life cycle and its equivalent version with technology, technology life cycle theory have been widely cited and applied to explain different phenomenon that required a flow of products and technologies from an origin to downward streams in different regions or markets.

In explaining phenomenon of technology marketing, the same theory

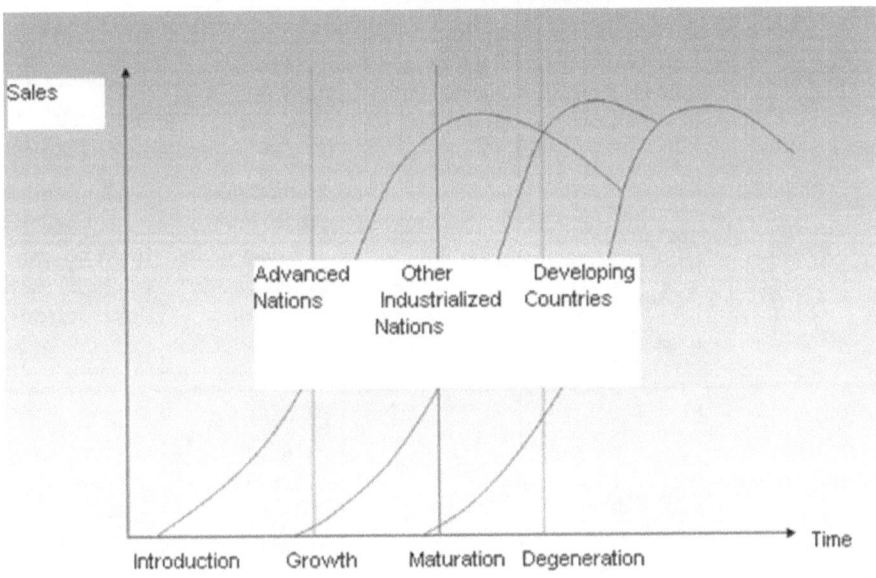

Figure 1-1 Technology Life Cycle [1]
(Source: Vernon, Raymond, 1966, International Investment and International Trade in the Product Cycle, Quarterly Journal of Economics 80, 190-207)

---

[1] Technology Life Cycle concept was first introduced by Vernon, and widely used as generically in many fields.

clearly shows strong explanatory power. Especially since the technology development cases dealt in this book are cases where technological gaps exist between the forerunners and catch-up seeking rivals, the theory gives a framework to see how the cases are behind vis-à-vis the leaders. Only difference would be the sequence. While the original theory tried to present a flow from the advanced to less developed regions or sectors, the reference model in this book is to view from the less developed side.

Despite the use of the technology life cycle theory, this book is not solely relying on the theory of life cycle alone. This book utilizes other theories like BCG matrix, other empirical research on time gap between leader and the followers, and theories on technology diffusion, which will together form a relatively well articulated picture.

	Introduction	Growth stage	Maturity stage	Decline stage
Revenue	Low level Slowly increases	Rapidly increase	Highest level/ Growth stalled	Diminishing
Profit	Low, due to advertisement and distribution costs	Profits surges with the increase of sales.	Maintaining certain level or diminished due to fierce market competition	Total profits are reduced, yet profit per unit can be increased due to scarcity.
Competition	Little competition	High level of competition due to entrance of competitiotors	Ologopoly is set up with withdrawal of weak competitors	Competitors exit from market
Production cost	high	diminishing	low	Very low

Consumer Characteristics	Consumer tastes are not diverse. Early adopter are main customers.	With competition introduced, consumer tastes diversify. Early adopters lead the market.	Diffusion of customers enlarge the range of choices.	Consumers with conservative tastes remain. Other consumers moved to other markets.
Promotional costs per customer	high	average	low	Very low
Marketing goal	Focus on enlarging the market. Try to let people buy	Increasing brand preference is the priority. Keeping up market share is also important.	Keeping market share and enlarging brand switching are the prioritized jobs,	Exit strategy to be excercised.

Table 1-1 Characteristics by stages of Technology life Cycle
(Source: Dunning, J.H. (2000b), 'The eclectic paradigm of international production: a personal perspective', in C. Pitelis and R. Sugden (eds), The Nature of the Transnational Firm, London: Routledge, pp. 119–39.; Vernon, Raymond, 1966, International Investment and International Trade in the Product Cycle, Quarterly Journal of Economics 80, 190-207)

In introduction stage, competition is limited due to almost no competition. At this stage, creating market would be an appropriate word for the innovator. Production cost is high, while, due to advertisement and distribution costs, profit is low and revenue is low yet slowly increasing. Consumers who would buy products and technology at this stage would be called the 'early adopters'. Promotional costs per consumer is high, and therefore marketing goal is to focus on enlarging the market and trying to let people buy.

At growth stage, with the increase of entrances or competing firms, competition level is hightened to a higher level. These rival firms, from their viewpoint, saw market potentials and success factors. Since demand for the product or technology takes off, production costs diminish rapidly together with sharp increase of revenue and profits. At this stage, consumers develop new tastes, led by early adopters. Marketing strategy would be to increase brand preference and keep up market shares.

As the product or technology reaches maturity stage, revenue reaches the highest moment, while profit diminishes with fierce competition. In market structure, oligopolitic structure is formed with some of the firms in the market leaving. Consumers have diverse tastes and choices, and marketing strategy is to keeping market share and enlarge brand switching.

Implications for international trade terms

The product life cycle in its original form presented by Raymond Vernon had its implications for international trade and international division of labor between different group of countries that are in different stages of economic development. From an innovating country's point of view, as technology life cycle or product life cycle, which almost overlap in this case, surges in growth stage, there is a portion for exports, since consumption for that product or technology is assumed to be constant. When the product or technology life cycle begins to turn downward in the mature stage, on the contrary, the innovating country should import the product or technology from the imitating countries, since there is some demand in the innovating country.

From an imitating country's point of view, since there is some domestic demand when the technology or product is in introduction stage in the innovating country, the product should be imported from the innovator. With technology transfer from innovator to imitator, the imitating country begins production, which results in export of the product or technology back to the innovator. While in figure 1-3, the imitator's technology life cycle is expressed as more like a S-curve, in typical description of Vernon style argument, the imitator's curve is another wave style replica of the innovator with time delays.

S-Curve model

Although the s-curve model is not a reference model in this analysis, it is usefule to review the core contents of the theory. This model is especially useful in explaining 'discontinuity' in technological progress and technology /product life cycles.[2] This model explains technology change as a shift from an existing S curve to a new S curve. In each S curve, there are three stages of embryonic, growth and maturity stages. As the stage progresses from embryonic to maturity, this model assumes that performance is enhanced. In this case, performance can be expressed as revenue for a specific product or technology.

What is interesting with this model is that it implies 'technology fatigue'. Any technology has a point of 'breakthrough' and a point of 'maximum R&D yield'. It is possible to find out that when nylon was about to be introduced, rayon still had strong potential to remain. The existing product generally tend to make technological extension like in the case of 'super rayon'. Yet, the market receives the new product. It is noteworthy that the cumulative R&D efforts expressed in U.S. dollars. Until the initial debut of a technology, huge sum of money is spent with still insufficient performance compared to the existing product or technology. After this hurdle, with relatively small amount of money, performance of the new product or technology can easily exceed the existing technology or product.

It is an insightful model, yet it is noteworthy that S-curve model is useful for descriptive analysis, but less useful for prescriptive analysis. Strategywise, established firms may have an advantage with component related S-curve changes, but attackers have advantage with architectural changes.

Technology Adoption Life Cycle Model

Technology adoption life cycle shows a proportional distribution of consumers adopting new products or technologies. In the cycle, innovators

---

[2] Walter Eversheim ed. Innovation Management for Technical Products: Systematic and Integrated product development and product planning Springer 2009

are followed by early adopters and early majority groups. Under the curve are late majority and laggards.[3]

Innovators can be called as techies, while early adopters can be renamed as 'visionaries'. Early majority group can be called as pragmatist, since they saw the feasibility from the early two groups and find there is no necessity to delay further.

	HIGH MARKET SHARE	**LOW MARKET SHARE**
High Growth Market	 High growth, high market share(STAR)	 High growth, low market share(QUESTION MARK)
Low growth Market	 Low growth, High market share(CASH COW)	 Low growth, low market share(DOG)

(Source:http://www.maxi-pedia.com/bcg+matrix+model)
Figure 1-2 BCG Matrix

In comparison, the late majority group is a conservative group.[4]

---

[3] Moore, G.A., 2006. Crossing the Chasm: Marketing and Selling Disruptive Products to Mainstream Customers. 3rd ed. New York: Harper Collins Publishers.

[4] Moore, G.A., 1991. Crossing the Chasm: Marketing and Selling High-Tech Products to Mainstream Customers. 2nd ed. New York: Harper Perennial.; Moore, G.A., 2006. Crossing the Chasm: Marketing and Selling Disruptive Products to Mainstream Customers. 3rd ed. New York: Harper Collins Publishers. ; Alicia Mullor-Sebastian., 1983. The Product Life Cycle Theory: Empirical Evidence Journal of International Business Studies Vol. 14, No. 3 (Winter, 1983), pp. 95-105

Technology Performance Life Cycle

There is a relaxed s-curve style figure named the technology performance life cycle in which performance limit is expressed with the passing of time and technology stage

BCG Matrixs

As a supplement to technology life cycle theory and its applications, this book utilizes the so-called 'BCG matrix'. The purpose of using this is to segmentize technologies in the identical stage in technology life cycles.

For example, two individual technologies both at maturity stage can be divided into one being a 'star' and the other being a 'dog' technology. Thus, it is to confer a new dimension to the existing technology typology based on cycles. Star technology indicates high growth, high market share technology, while cow denotes low growth, high market share technology.

Moore's Technology Life Cycle

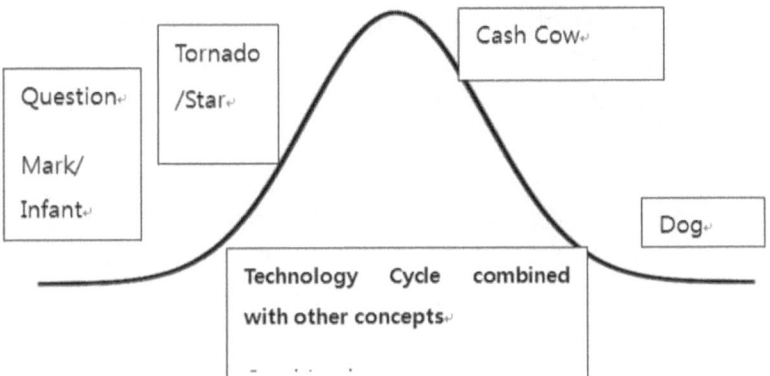

Figure 1-3 Technology Cycles in Summary
(Modified with other concepts and applied from: Geoffrey A. Moore, *Inside the Tornado* Collins.2005.)

With figure 1-3, it is possible to overlap concepts and theories discussed in one chart. Technology adoption cycle can be positioned in the earlier part of a product life cycle for the first time adopters. Product life cycle is much longer in the sense that seemingly outdated products or technologies sometimes find their 'second life' in the long right hand side tail. The classic model of Technology Adoption Life Cycle (TALC) was presented in the book, Diffusion of Innovations by Rogers in 1962. The core idea was that individuals adopt innovation and its products at different rates over time instead of adopting it at the same time.

Upon the earlier discussion on the adoption cycle, Moore explained that there is a critical difference between early adopters and the early majority regarding their justification for buying new innovation products. The early adopters are looking for a change agent, taking the emerging technology as a strategic business opportunity. In comparison, early majority wants incremental productivity improvement.

Moore further elaborated the TALC in his 1995 book, 'Inside the Tornado', in which the author presented three marketing stages on the other side of The Chasm within the early majority category: The Bowling Alley, The Tornado, and Main Street. Implication form the book was that business strategies must be changed fundamentally as new innovation products pass through the stages.

* The Bowling Alley: In this stage, a new product gets acceptance from niches within the early majority market, yet it has not achieved widespread and rapid adoption. This niche market represents a steady profitable business, and the niche customers can become a valuable reference source to promote the product to the mainstream market.

* The Tornado: The tornado shows the rapid adoption of a new product by the early majority market, which is graphed with increasingly steeply upward part of the technology adoption curve. Psychological nature of the early majority works in the mechanism, in which members tend to take calculated risks only. When the the alpha risk is the risk to switching too early, while the beta risk is the risk of switching too late, pragmatists would want to minimize alpha and beta risks by buying altogether as a group, buying from a market leader, and completing the transition as

soon as possible. The consequence is a rapid growth, during which market leadership and industry standards are set.

For discussion purpose, the BCG group style grouping is added to the curve for understanding.

Technology Development cooperation satges

Technology development cases discussed in this book cover university—local government—SMEs(small & medium enterprises) networks. In this web, there are multiple stages, in which different expectations and arrangements are possible.

Pre-competition			Competition stage				
R&D cooperation			Technical cooperation			Manufacturing/ Marketing cooperation	
A	B	C	D	E	F	G	H
Univ. centered research funded by private entities	Gov't-industry cooperation project in which univ and public research institutions participate	arrangement based on private firms	a venture capital investment within a big company	a non-equity technological arrangement between firms on selective areas	inter-firm technical arrangement which includes a multiple types of cross licensing of technology	a joint venture or a comprehensive R&D, manufacturing, and marketing consortium	a licensing agreement or marketing arrangement

Table 1-2 Technology Development Cooperation stages
(Source: adopted from OECD OECD Science, Technology and Industry Outlook 2012, 2014)

In pre-competition stage, the form of cooperation is R&D oriented. There can be at least three types under this category. The first one, type A, would be a university research funded by private entities. In this case, public endowment is not necessarily involved. Type B is a government- industry cooperation project in which university and public research institutions participate. Type C shows an arrangement based on private firms.

As the stage turns into competition stage, the nature of cooperation is shifted. Competition stage can be divided into two separate stages: Technical cooperation and Manufacturing/ Marketing cooperation. In technical cooperation, it is possible to distinguish three sub types. As column D shows, the first type under technical cooperation is a venture capital investment within a big company. It could be invested by multiple stakeholders. Column E shows a non-equity technological arrangement between firms on selective areas. Column F is a inter-firm technical arrangement which includes a multiple types of cross licensing of technology and products.

As the stage changes into the next level, Type G shows a joint venture or a comprehensive R&D, manufacturing, and marketing consortium. Finally, column H presents a licensing agreement or marketing arrangement.

Time Gap between the leader and followers

As an example to show how fast developed technologies can be diffused to their rival firms, an empirical research was conducted with 100 firms in 13 industries, which reported that pivotal decisions on manufacturing process, technology development or technologies and products can be in the hands of rivals as shorts 12 to 18 months (Mansfield). A critical implication from this study is that if developing a technology and putting it into the market takes more than three years, the technology development is becoming useless or in a lesser painful word, less meaningful.

This is a critieria used in this book in evaluating the time between the leader and the followers in the following chapters. Perhaps the three year gap would be a critical bar. As one sees in the table 1-3 below, there is a percentage distribution of how many months would it take until rival firms can know what you have decided on major new products or processes in ten major sectors in the U.S.

	Products				
	6 months or less	Between 6-12 months	Between 12-18 months	18 months or longer	Row Total 1)
Chemical	18	36	9	36	100

Pharmaceutical	57	14	29	0	100
Petroleum	22	33	22	22	100
First iron	40	20	0	40	100
Electric	38	50	12	0	100
Machinery	31	31	31	8	100
Transportation equipment	25	50	0	25	100
Tools	50	38	12	0	100
Glass, stone	40	60	0	0	100
Others	31	15	15	38	100
Average	35	35	13	17	
	Process				
Chemical	0	0	10	90	100
Pharmaceutical	0	33	0	67	100
Petroleum	10	50	10	30	100
First Iron	40	40	0	20	100
Electric	14	14	57	14	100
Machinery	10	20	30	40	100
Transportation equipment	0	67	0	33	100
Tools	33	33	33	0	100
Glass, stone	0	20	20	60	100
others2)	27	0	36	36	100
Average	13	28	20	39	100

Table 1-3 Time Gap between the leader and followers
(Source: adopted from OECD **OECD Science, Technology and Industry Outlook 2012, 2014**)
* 1981 data for 100 firms that used more than 1 million U.S. dollars in R&D or revenue exceeding 85 million US dollars and spending more than 1% of the revenue in R&D

1) Due to rounding, row total may not be 100%.
2) Metal processing, food/ beverage, paper products are included in others category.

One key to note is that in most sectors, if one adds up the percentage for '6 months or less' and between 6 and 12 months, the figure is usually 50% or higher.

Process showed a little different distribution in terms of average months, yet generalization that one can get is identical as in the case of products.

Sectors of innovation origin and users of innovation

Another interesting dimension in the study of technology development and innovation diffusion is where those innovations are utilized. Based on a survey research of U.S. industry, interesting findings can be presented with the table in the below. With a time frame from 1945 to 1983, the research has given us insights on the followings.

	Innovation Used where It was originated	Innovation Used in Other Manufacturing sectors	Innovation Used in Non-Manufacturing sectors	Percentage of top 3 sectors where innovation was used
Machinery	14.2	58.1	27.7	Textile (19.8)
				manufacturing (11.5)
				electronics (10.2)
Chemical	24.9	32.1	43.0	Health (24.9)
				Textile (13.1)
				agriculture (6.3)
Tools	9.9	47.9	42.2	Textile (9.9)
				R&D (9.7)
				HEALTH (8.4)
Electronics	37.4	11.7	50.9	Defense (10.1)
				Office ware (8.4)
				R&D (7.6)
Total	30.5	34.0	35.5	

Table 1-4 Sectors of innovation origin and users of innovation (1945~83) (Source: adopted from OECD **OECD Science, Technology and Industry Outlook 2012, 2014**)

First, with an exception of electronics, most innovation is used outside the sector or field where it was developed. Second, service sectors are heavily indebted to innovations coming from various sectors. Third, health sector is clearly assisted by chemical and tools sectors. Electronics sector's influence on defense sector has inescapable. Although the time frame for the research was ended in 1980s, it is quite clear similar patterns would be maintained, considering chain-like linkage between sectors.

Korean Electronics: strong and weak points

This book takes examples of technology development form the Korean electronics cases, where university and firms cooperate with some local funding. Easily perceived image of the Korean electronics sector is that their government competitiveness is high. A closer look, however, would reveal that there are strong and weak points. With the existence of the weak points, the rationale for starting the cooperative R&D projects could have been found.

In the table below, Korean electronics firms have accumulated considerable amount of achievements. Samsung and Hynix have been achieving their milestones in semi conductor areas, while at the same time Samsung's another subsidiary and LG-Philips have been leaders in LCD and OLED technology. These movements in technology development are, in fact, sufficient enough to assume that they are quite well established in most areas in finishing electronics products.

Firm	item	Contents of development
Samsung	Semi Conductor	2006.04 Next gen.package: (WSP) development 2006.05 Hybrid HDD prototype 2006.09 Intelligent DDI 2006.09 40 nano 32 giga Nand Flash
Samsung	LCD	2005.03 82" TFT LCD 2005.05 40" OLED for TVs 2005.10 color filterless 32" LCD 2005.11 plastic flexible TFT LCD

Samsung SDI	PDP OLED	2004.12 102" full HD class PDP 2005.11 4th gen. AM OLED mass production investment 2006.07 dual slim AM OLED
LG Eletronics	PDP	2005.07 full HD class 60" PDP 2005.08 50" HD class single scan PDP 2006.08 60" single scan PDP module
LG-Philips LCD	AM OLED LCD	2004.10 20.1" low temperature poly AM OLED 2005.05 47" LED backlight LCD 2006.03 100" LCD
Hynix	Semi conductor	2005.01 Single Fab capacity of 100,000 units per months 2006.03 80 nano DDR2 commercial mass production 2006.07 single Fab capacity of 140,000 units per months

Table 1-5 Major milestones of semiconductor industry of Korea
(Source: Gyunggi Pride Research Unit Report 2007)

As seen in the table 1-5, Korean electronics industry is one of the major global suppliers of cellular phones. Yet, the Korean industry has been importing key parts as well as material used in the phone manufacturing, which has costed them more than a few billion U.S. dollars annually as of 2004-2007 period. Technology development projects introduced in this book was to reduce import reliance for the cell phone manufacturing process, in which university research manpower has been engaged in.

Gen \ Types	1	2	2.5	3	3.5		4
Type	Analog	CDMA GSM	CDMA 2001 IX	CDMA 2000 IX EV-DV	WCDMA	HSDPA	HSUPA	3GLTE MBWA MOBILE Wimax EVO
Data Transmission speed	n/a	9.6-64 Kbps	144Kbps	download 2.4Mbps upload 144Kbps	download 2Mbps upload 384Kbps	download 14Mbps upload 1.4Mbps	download 14Mbps upload 5.8Mbps	100Mbps
service	voice	Short messag	photo bell sound	High Speed movies	Slow, Video Phone function	Smooth Video phone	Multiple Mobile gaming	High Capacity multi Media Contents

availibility	1984	1996.1	2000.10	2002.2	2003.12	2006.6	Late 2007	2010

Table 1-6 Generational division of cell phones
(Source: Gyunggi Pride Research Unit Report 2007)

Scope of the Book

Chapter one of this book has discussed on theoretical contents that will be the basis for discussion in this book. In chapter one, this book has reviewed a range of technology life cycle based theories as a reference for technology evaluation from a marketing point of view. Chapter two will present trends of IT technology development, followed by technology evaluation in chapter 3, in which evaluation was conducted in a dual track method: those of inside and outside evaluation.

After chapter 3, chapter 4 will analyze technology trend and the world market with a focus on cell phone related markets, since the theme of technology development, which his micro packaging has very close linkage to the absolute size of the cell phone markets and its shaping over the years.

Following from the lineage of discussion, chapter 5 will emphasize the importance of demand side by showing 'failure cases' of technologically successful, but market wisely failed technology cases. Although the coverage of technologies in IT field was not extensive enough to draw generalization and the covered cases relied on 'availability heuristic in searching for cases, which means that there could be some bias, yet this chapter is enough to 'alarm' the salience' of the market forces in action. Finally a concluding chapter will wind up the discussion in the book.

CHAPTER 2

TRENDS OF IT TECHNOLOGY DEVELOPMENT

1. Technology Aspects

This chapter will look through technology development trend, especially related to cellular phone manufacturing. In the figure 2-1 below, bar charts show total broadband market size with sub divided composition of the market. With access market taking the lion's share, services and contents markets follow in terms of the composition, and device part takes the smallest section.

As have briefly mentioned, since Korea's electronics industry has been focusing on finalized device orientation, while recent developments also show its entry into software and other areas, the degrees of freedom the industry could rejoice have been tightly dwindled since its entry into the world cell phone market.

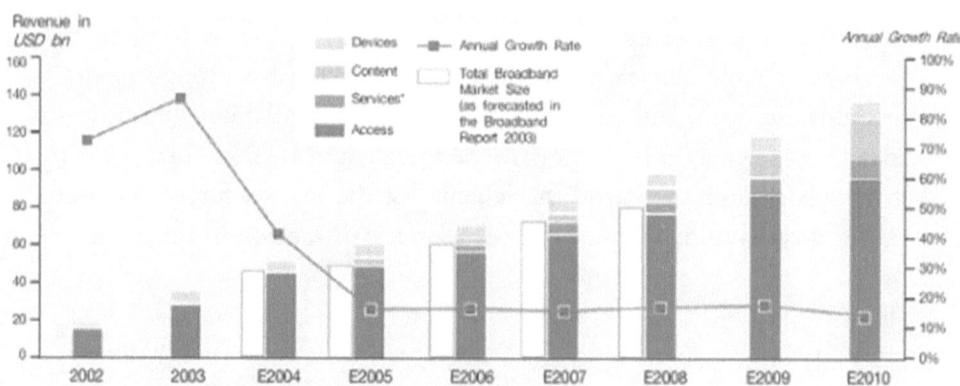

Figure 2-1 Annual Growth of Electronics Market
(source: Techno Systems Research Co., Ltd. 2006; Junmo Kim Gyunggi Pride Report)

In addition to the sheer numbers that show the relatively smaller chunk of the total broadband market, what has been molestering the sector was its reliance on imported parts. This chapter focuses on some of the part development cases within the scope of cell phone parts. Before this chapter starts looking into the trend of technology development, it is essential to mention that the most important technology trend in cell phone manufacturing has been 'packaging' of key parts, or micro packaging. Korean cell phone manufacturing industry, with its small and medium size supply chain firms, have suffered lack of technology and integration in the fields.

In packaging technology trend, especially in micro packaging, 'reflow packaging' has been the main stream as of 2004, and is expected to show some growth by 2014.

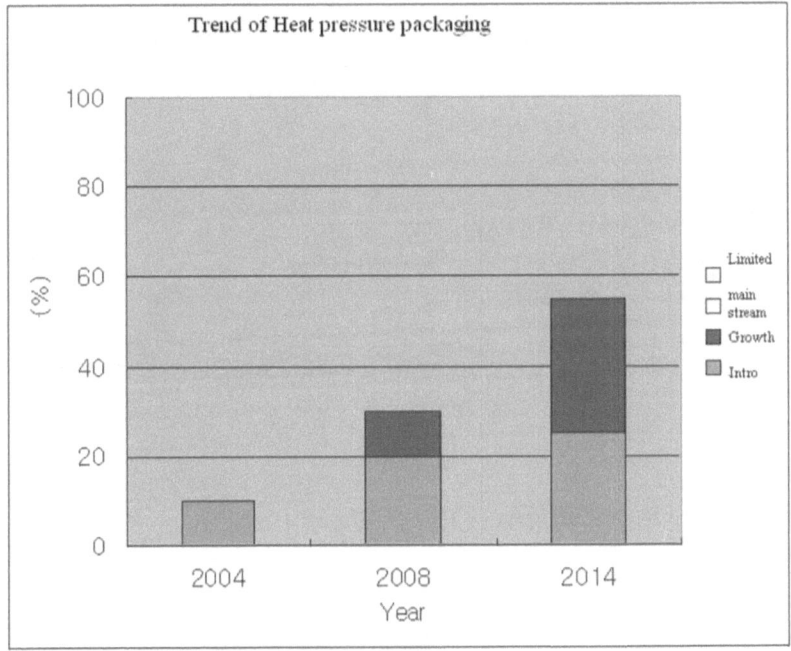

Figure 2-2 Trend of heat pressure packaging
(Source: Korea micro joining research coop 2007)

Regarding 'heat pressure packaging', the industry showed introduction of the technology as of year 2004, and continued with growth from 2008 onward. It has been expected to show continued growth in 2014. In comparison, the relatively new technology, 'conductive adhesive' packaging has entered the market in 2008 with expectation to enter the growth stage by 2014.

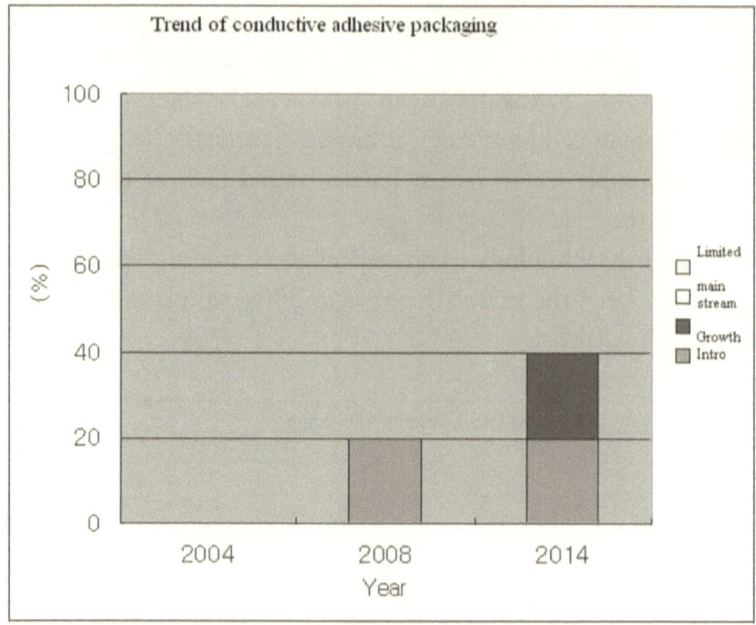

Figure 2-3 Trend of Conductive Adhesive packaging
(Source: Korea micro joining research coop 2007)

In table 2-3, it is possible to examine the industry trend in numbers, which highlight where packaging trend is going in terms of numbers.

Importance of packaging

Power, heat, and impurities the package. With layers get thinner in semiconductor manufacturing, very fine 45nm and 32nm with microprocessors and FPGAs — high power chips are the early adopters of that technology —have a lot of leads with flip chip-type packaging. The material used is generally porous and fragile, which impacts the packaging. When this kind of a low-k dielectric is processed with the standard wire bonding technique, the material under the bonding pad must be selected carefully since the standard bonding force may crack the dielectric, which could bring reliability problems.

On the other hand, if flip chip packaging is used, which involves putting solder bumps on the die, heat can cause issues with low-k dielectric. Since the industry has been shifting away from lead for the solder bumps to non-lead-type materials, there is a need to reduce the melting point of the solder by changing the type of materials. Furthermore, when die is cut apart on the wafers, the sawing process tends to leave behind a tough edge. In the past, it was not a problem, yet with low-k dielectric roughness can cause a crack that will affect the whole die. As a result, structures have been added to the scribe area in between the die area on the wafer to resist the propagation of the cracks.

The second problem with current and next generation semiconductor packaging is electromigration of the copper. Particularly with flip chip attachment where solder is being applied to the die, the tin in the solder can diffuse and form intermetallics, which causes reliability issues because when current is run through it. Sometimes voids in the metal conductors increase current densities. Solution for this is using copper bumps on the die instead of just putting the solder directly on the die such as under-bump metallization (UBM) structures.

AS the third problem, thermal issues have been an undying issue, particularly for microprocessors and FPGAs. Heat gives packaging industry a way to control the heat out, while package makers keep striving to develop thermally enhanced packages.

A new trend in packaging would be the 3D packaging, in which chips are thinned, stacked and interconnected increase density and performance. This way saves a lot of power so that terabit per second memory bandwidth can be supplied using die stacked on top of the processor with 2 to 5 watts of power instead of 25 to 30 watts going through the existing package." 3D packaging is still under development and expected to be seen first in CPUs because of the intensity of the problems to solve.

Yet, additional issues arise with this approach including the need to thin the die. Given that the low-k approach causes fragility, traditional thinning techniques can crush the fragile layers. One of the solutions is to include the use of chemical etching, reactive ion etching. IBM and AMD are using silicon on insulator (SOI) technology, which uses silicon dioxide in the process, which is easier to perform the thinning since chemicals used to etch silicon will not erode silicon dioxide.

Technical terms & Trends in packaging methods

Fine-pitch BGA(FBGA) packages are near chip-size versions of the ball-grid array family, featuring smaller, thinner dimensions and flexible body size and pincount availability. They are assembled using shared tooling and common substrate panels allowing new package sizes to be created with far less cost and lead-times than conventional packaging. A QFP or Quad Flat Package is an integrated circuit package with leads at four sides, which is used primarily for surface mounting (SMD). There are versions having from 32 to over 200 pins with a pitch ranging from 0.4 to 1.0 mm, while some special cases include LQFP (Low profile QFP) and TQFP (Thin QFP).

The QFP package type has become common in Europe and US during the early nineties, while QFP components have been used in Japanese consumer electronics since the seventies. A package related to QFP is called PLCC, which is similar but has pins with larger pitch, 1.27 mm (or 1/20 inch) with curve underneath a thicker body to simplify socketing.

The basic form is a flat rectangular (often square) body with pins at four sides but with numerous variation in the design. These differ usually only in pin number, pitch, dimensions, and materials used (usually to improve thermal characteristics). A clear variation is Bumpered Quad Flat Package with extensions at the four corners to protect the pins against mechanical damage before the unit is soldered.

Examples of the some of variations of QFP are as follows.

BQFP: Bumpered Quad Flat Package
BQFPH: Bumpered Quad Flat Package with heat spreader
CQFP: Ceramic Quad Flat Package
FQFP: Fine Pitch Quad Flat Package
HQFP: Heat sinked Quad Flat Package
LQFP: Low Profile Quad Flat Package
MQFP: Metric Quad Flat Package
PQFP: Plastic Quad Flat Package
SQFP: Small Quad Flat Package

TQFP: Thin Quad Flat Package
VQFP: Very small Quad Flat Package
VTQFP: Very Thin Quad Flat Package

Some QFP packages have an Exposed Pad. The exposed pad is an extra pad underneath or on top of the QFP that may act as a ground connection and/or as a heat sink for the package.

FLGA is a laminate substrate based package with plastic overmolded encapsulation. Different from a standard FBGA, second level interconnect is achieved on the LGA by connecting "lands" on the package directly onto the PCB through solder re-flow. The elimination of solder balls brings better electrical performance and lower package profile without using the more expensive thinner BT core material. It also offers the flexibility of land pattern arrangement in the form of signal lands or heat spreader/ground pads to suit the thermal and electrical requirements of various devices. The FLGA package's reduced outline and thickness make it an ideal advanced technology packaging solution for high performance and/or portable applications.

The QFN package is a thermally enhanced standard size IC package designed to eliminate the use of bulky heat sinks and slugs. This package can be easily mounted using standard PCB assembly techniques and can be removed and replaced using standard repair procedures. The QFN package is designed so that the lead frame die pad (or thermal pad) is exposed on the bottom of the IC (see Figure 1). This provides an extremely low thermal resistance ($\square JC$) path between the die and the exterior of the package. The QFN (RGY) package has the same pin out as the thin scale small outline packages (TSSOP), yet, it is up to 62% smaller than the TSSOP. Based on QFN modeling research outcomes, thermal performance is improved up to 55% and electrical performance (inductance and capacitance) improved up to 60% and up to 30% respectively over the TSSOP package. Product designers are able to take advantage of reduced form factors in personal digital assistants, cell phones, and other portable consumer electronics by using this package.

Item			2004	2008	2014
# of LSI used(counting 16 pin or higher)		Cell phone	8~17	5~15	5~10
# of LSI used(counting 16 pin or higher)		DVC	5~30	10~20	5~15
% of packages used	QFP/SOP	Cell Phone	5	5	0
% of packages used	QFP/SOP	DVC	35	20	20
% of packages used	FBGA	Cell phone	75	80	87
% of packages used	FBGA	DVC	50	60	60
% of packages used	FLGA	Cell phone	5	5	5
% of packages used	FLGA	DVC	10	13	10
% of packages used	QFN	Cell phone	15	10	5
% of packages used	QFN	DVC	5	7	10
Minimum pitch in packaging (mm)	QFP/SOP	Cell phone	0.4~0.5	0.4	-
Minimum pitch in packaging (mm)	QFP/SOP	DVC	0.4	0.4	0.4
Minimum pitch in packaging (mm)	FBGA	Cell phone	0.4~0.5	0.3~0.4	0.3
Minimum pitch in packaging (mm)	FBGA	DVC	0.4	0.4	0.3

Technology Development and Marketing

Minimum pitch in packaging (mm)	FLGA	Cell phone	0.65	0.4–0.5	0.3–0.4
Minimum pitch in packaging (mm)	FLGA	DVC	0.65	0.5	0.4
Minimum pitch in packaging (mm)	QFN	Cell phone	0.4–0.5	0.4	0.4
Minimum pitch in packaging (mm)	QFN	DVC	0.5	0.5	0.5
Max # of pins in package	QFP/SOP	Cell phone	50–80	100	–
Max # of pins in package	QFP/SOP	DVC	120	80	64
Max # of pins in package	FBGA	Cell phone	200–600	300–600	600
Max # of pins in package	FBGA	DVC	400	600	800
Max # of pins in package	FLGA	Cell phone	300	400	500
Max # of pins in package	FLGA	DVC	250	300	300
Max # of pins in package	QFN	Cell phone	20–60	80	100
Max # of pins in package	QFN	DVC	64	64	64
Minimum height to mount in packaging (including multichips) (mm)	QFP/SOP	Cell phone	1.0	0.8	–

Minimum height to mount in packaging (including multichips) (mm)	QFP/SOP	DVC	1.2	0.8	0.8
Minimum height to mount in packaging (including multichips) (mm)	FBGA	Cell phone	1.0–1.4	0.8–1.0	0.5–0.8
Minimum height to mount in packaging (including multichips) (mm)	FBGA	DVC	1.2	0.8	0.8
Minimum height to mount in packaging (including multichips) (mm)	FLGA	Cell phone	1.0	0.8	0.5
Minimum height to mount in packaging (including multichips) (mm)	FLGA	DVC	1.0	0.6	0.6

| Minimum height to mount in packaging (including multichips) (mm) | QFN | Cell phone | 1.0 | 0.8 | 0.5 |
| Minimum height to mount in packaging (including multichips) (mm) | QFN | DVC | 1.2 | .08 | 0.8 |

Table 2-1 Forecast of packaging ratio
(Source: Korea micro joining research coop 2007)

Some of the implications from the technology trend can be presented as follows.

- Percentage of packages used in cell phones and DVCs in QFP/SOP, FBGA, FLGA, QFN packages tend toincrease over the years.
- The number of LSI used(counting 16 pin or higher) in cell phones and DVCs also tend to be increased.
- Minimum pitch in packaging (mm) in cell phones and DVCs in QFP/SOP, FBGA, FLGA, QFN packages tend to be decreased over the coming years.
- Maximum number of pins in QFP/SOP, FBGA, FLGA, QFN packages tend to grow over the years in the near future.
- Minimum height to mount in packaging is expected to decrease through the coming years.

Trends in Bare Chips

Physical designs and performance requirements of most chips are not conducive to stacking. Examples of these limitations can be summarized as follows.

First, problem of escaping I/O from stacked die identical in size and I/O assignment exists.

Second, when I/O have been wired out to the edges of stacked chips, they then must be wired down the side of the stack to the next level of interconnect.

Third, most chips only have one active surface and, therefore they have only one route of wiring escape.

Finally, the active surface of most chips has little or no passivation protection, and Bare chip approach is very clearly expected to expand into between 10 most nitride/oxide barrier levels are fragile. This means there is a significant chance of damage to the chip during the stacking process. to 50% by 2014. Wire bonding seems to have shown limitations. In line with the trend, minimum pad pitch of bare chips is being reduced as a projection from technological development. So is the minimum thickness of bare chips. Costwisely, bare chip approach clearly gives a sharp reduction of costs.

Item		2004	2008	2014
% of bare chip packaging		5	5–20	10–50
Flip chip bonding		○	○	○
Wire bonding		×	×	×
Minimum pad pitch of bare chips (FCB)	peripherals	50	50	10–30
Minimum pad pitch of bare chips (FCB)	Area array	150–200	150–200	80–100
minimum thickness of bare chips (mm)		200	70–100	25–50

Types of bare chips		wafer	Tray wafer	Tape wafer
Costs (compared to package %)	KGD Known Good die	100	80~90	50~90
Costs (compared to package %)	Non-KGD	70	50~60	50~60

Table 2-2 Forecast of Bare chip use
(Source: Korea Micro Joining Research Coop 2007)

Trends in System-on-Chips

System-on-a-chip (SOC) and System-in-a-package (SIP) are used in a wide range of electronic products including cell phones, MP3 players, digital televisions, television set-top boxes, PCs, gaming consoles, and other wireless communication devices.

item	2004	2008	2014
Requirements for System on chip	Low costs, reduced development cycles, Stability (quality control) Verification tools Tools for interpretation of bad chips Estimation of development costs		
Requirements for System-in-a-package (SIP)	Low costs, reduced development cycles, Stability (quality control) Verification tools LSI venders should secure Known good die(KGD). Securing quality assurance system between chip manufacturer and packaging firm / and between packaging firm and sales company		

Table 2-3 Requirements for SOC/SIP
(Source: Korea micro joining research coop 2007)

item			2004	2008	2012
Chip condensor Chip resistor Chip inductor	Max size W × D	cell phone	3.2 × 1.6	2.0 × 1.25	1.0 × 0.5
Chip condensor Chip resistor Chip inductor	Max size W × D	DVC	3.2 × 1.6	3.2 × 1.6	2.0 × 1.25
Chip condensor Chip resistor Chip inductor	Min size W × D	cell phone	0.6 × 0.3	0.4 × 0.2	0.4 × 0.2
Chip condensor Chip resistor Chip inductor	Min size W × D	DVC	0.6 × 0.3	0.6 × 0.3	0.4 × 0.2
Chip condenser Max size	D × W × H	cell phone	7.3×4.3×2.8	6×3.2×2.5	3.2×1.6×1.6
Chip condenser Max size	D × W × H	DVC	3.2×2.5×6.0	3.2×2.5×6.0	2.0×1.25×2
Chip condenser Max size	aluminium DΦ × H	cell phone DVC	Not used		
Error margin In Chip parts (mm)	exterior	cell phone DVC	0.01	0.005	0.005
Error margin In Chip parts (mm)	electrode	cell phone DVC	0.015	0.005	0.003

Table 2-4 Forecast for Chip dimension requirements unit: mm
(Source: Korea Micro Joining Research Coop 2007)

Technology Development and Marketing

Trends in Environmental Adaptation

Micro packaging is not an exception in terms of applying environmental policy consideration. Showing this concern, micro packaging area can be projected with several items listed in the below.

First, with the time frame from 2004 to 2014, % of recycled packaging material in cell phone is expected to rise from 20% to 100% by 2014. Likewise, in DVC, the percentage of using recycled packaging would reach 100% during the same time frame.

item					2004	2008	2012
% of bulk case packaging	cell phone				0 ~ 10	30 ~ 40	50 ~ 100
% of bulk case packaging	DVC				5 ~ 10	15 ~ 20	20 ~ 50
% of bulk case packaging	cell phone DVC				-quality maintenance of electrodes -Tape resistance - ways to meet multi type, small orders -reliability of electrode		
Bulk case requirements	Recycling requirements				Decomposability of Recycled parts Eco friendliness of recycling		
Environmental Policy issue	% of recycled packaging material		cell phone		20 ~ 50	50 ~ 100	100
Environmental Policy issue	% of recycled packaging material		DVC		10 ~ 90	100	100
Environmental Policy issue)	% of recycled packaging material	tray	cell phone		20 ~ 50	50 ~ 100	100

Environmental Policy issue	% of recycled packaging material	tray	DVC	10 ~ 100	100	100
Environmental Policy issue	% of recycled packaging material	Bulk case	cell phone	20 ~ 50	50 ~ 100	100
Environmental Policy issue	% of recycled packaging material	Bulk case	DVC	100	100	100

Table 2-5 Trends in Environmental Adpatation
(Source: Korea Micro Joining Research Coop 2007)

Summary of the future trend in micro packaging

This section of chapter 2 has reviewed technological trends in micro packaging fields. While different technological possibilities were presented, the 3D packaging would show more potential for the future. 3D packaging, which is still under development, yet it is clearly a new trend, with which chips are thinned, stacked and interconnected increase density and performance. Below are some of the new requirements or directions for packaging.

- Slim, high definition, flexible display

- slimness in camera module design (slimness in optical part)

- Compatibility and interface with home networking, RFID, UWB, and biometrics, voice-input, automatic translation

Wearable PCs

- low cost, multi-stacking micro printing of lines (10 layers with lines less than 0.6mm)

-built-in-multi functions

Technology Development and Marketing

-low temperature, high density packaging
- very thinness between layers (layer interval between 40μm~60μm) thatenables high speed transmission
- new packaging that does not use PCB
- energy saving media drive
Requirments for semiconductors and packaging
- Securing reliability of multipin-dense pitch packaging without underfills
- Improved anti-shock capability under lead free packaging
- low voltage operation and ESD response $3.0V \rightarrow 1.5V \rightarrow 0.8V \rightarrow 0.5V$
- Low cost packaging   current 100% → 2006년 70% → 2012년 50%
- Thinness in packaging   from 0.8mm → to 0.5mm
-large scale memory   stacked chip/3 D memory package/PoP preparation
-One chip cell phone
- low cost KGD chip in packaging
- bad sector detection in non-destruction scanning of FBGA/FLGA
- highly effective heat emission method in 3 D packaging
High capacity of battery
During operation(typical): 300mW, waiting: 3mW Ultra low consumption of electricity, low electricity consumption of communication module High capacity and smaller size of battery

Ultra high density packaging, post- SMT packaging
Flexible, multi stack, low cost, PCB
Innovation in testing

Table 2-6 Technology Requirements for wireless devices
(Source: Korea Micro Joining Research Coop 2007)

2. Forecasting the Market Size
2.1. Electronics Packaging market: Cell Phone case

Based on techno systems research data, world market size for micro electronics packaging was around 7.5 billion U.S. dollars in 2006, 12.2 billion U.S. dollars in 2008. In comparison, the Korean market size was 120 million U.S. dollars in 2006, and 199 million U.S. dollars in 2008. Relative proportion of the Korean market in world market was 1.6% in 2006, and 1.63% in 2008 respectively.

	Market size (2006)	Market size (2008)
World market size	7.5 billion US dollars	12.2 billion US dollars
Korean market size	120 million US dollars	199 million US dollars

Table 2-7 Electronics packaging market: cell phone case
(source: Techno Systems Research Co., Ltd. 2006)

In the same years of 2006 and 2008, electronic packaging market Size for the flat display panels was in the below, in which the Korean market size was around 1% of the total world market size with round ups. This has been one of the key reason why technology development has been negelected, for firms would see this as a barren field. On the other hand, this could have been a 'virgin' field where new entrants can catch-up with the existing ones.

Technology Development and Marketing

	Market size (2006)	Market size (2008)
World market size	35,150 hundred million won 3.5 billion U.S. dollars	41,700 hundred million won 4.1 billion U.S. dollars
Korean market size	243 hundred million won 24.3 million U.S. dollars	315 hundred million won 31.5 million U.S. dollars

Table 2-8 Electronics packaging market size for Flat Display Panels
(source: Techno Systems Research Co., Ltd. 2006)

With the technology development efforts being evaluated in this book, it was expected that the following performance increase in revenue of regional firms and increase of incoming firms with investment.

	(2009) (1 year after technology development project)	(2010) (2 years after technology development project)	(2011) (3 years after technology development project)
Revenue increase in regional firms	0.4 billion U.S. dollars	0.5 billion U.S. dollars	0.8 billion U.S. dollars
# of firms invited to the region for investment	5	10	13

Table 2-9 Economic Impacts of micro packaging technology
(unit: 100 million won) (source: GyungGi 'PRIDE' research unit Report)
(Source: Korea Micro Joining Research Coop 2007)

2.2. Forecasting for Electronics packaging Material development

As a key component in cell phone manufacturing, Flexible Printed Circuit Board or Flexible circuit can be defined as a printed circuit pattern using a layer of copper foil over a polymer base. Polymer material is also used as the insulator for the exposed circuit pattern. Being made of all flexible materials, it allows the flexible circuit to be multidimensional.

It provides nearly unlimited adaptability for electrical connections between component parts. Flexible circuits can move, bend and twist without damage to the conductor. Flexible circuitry also allows conformity to different shapes.

A single sided flex circuit (basic) consists of a flexible polymer film laminated to a thin piece of copper. It is then chemically etched to produce a circuit pattern. Patterns can be created on both sides of the substrate film (double sided) with via plated-through holes. The vias are to make electrical connections between the two layers. A covercoat made of polymer is added to insulate the copper foil.

연차 적요	unit 단위	estimates			Est.	Forecast			
		2003	2004	2005	2006	2007	2008	2009	2010
quantity	t	950	1,700	2,900	3,940	3,840	4,510	5,320	6,290
% compared to last yr	%	-	178.9	170.6	135.9	97.5	117.4	118.0	117.7
Amount	Million yen	8,690	12,960	19,610	25,260	27,340	29,920	32,820	35,880
% compared to last yr	%	-	149.1	151.3	128.8	108.2	109.4	109.7	109.3
Avr price	yen/kg	9,100	7,600	6,800	6,400	7,100	6,600	6,200	5,700

Table 2-10 FPCB Market Forecast
(Source: Korea Micro Joining Research Coop 2007)

Looking at table 2-10, market for FPCB is expected to grow continuously through 2010. Yet, reflecting a typical mass production characteristic, the unit price has been reduced by 30% comparing the prices in 2003 and 2010. Another interesting finding is that in Figure 2-10, one can note that the amount of FPCB sold and the volume of the product have shown a closely proportionate relationship, which signifies that the unit price decrease was, as a hindsight, quite appropriate to reflect a healthy market growth typical in many mass market examples and technology life cycle theory.

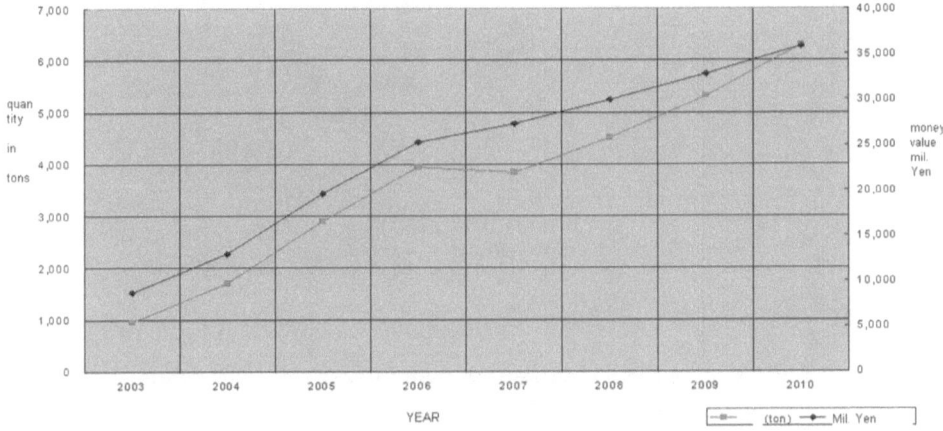

Figure 2-4 FPCB Market forecast: quantity & sales volume
(source: Display industry analysis, KISTEP 2005)

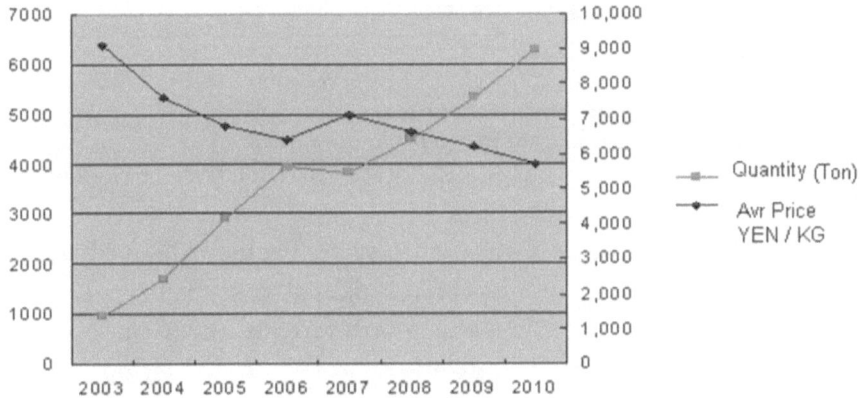

Figure 2-5 FPCB Market Forecast: quantity & Average price
(source: Display industry analysis, KISTEP 2005)

In comparison, Figure 2-5 shows a typical reverse relationship between quantity increase and decrease of unit costs, which is a healthy evidence for the growth of the market. This scissor like figure just explains the same phenomenon explained with the previous figure.

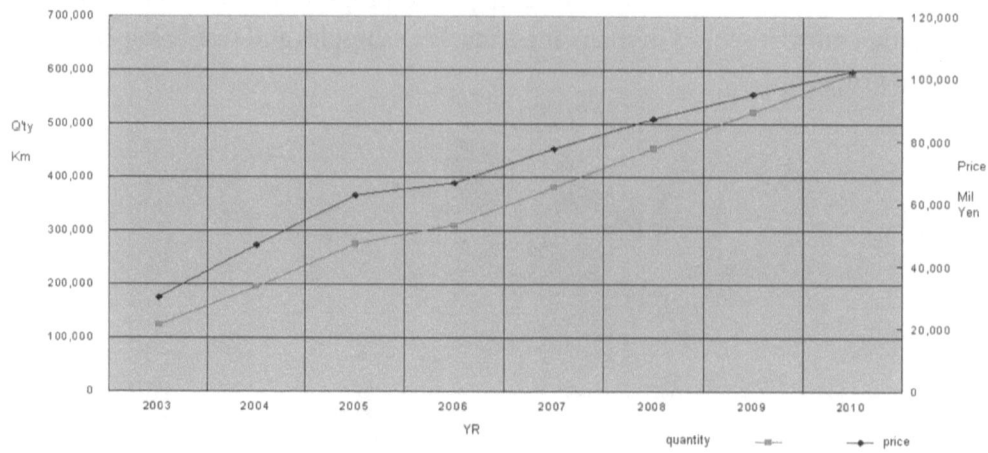

Figure 2-6 Plotting of FPCB Market forecast: quantity & sales volume
(source: Display industry analysis, KISTEP 2005)

	(2009)	(2010)	(2011)
Firm revenue increase	5 billion won	7 billion won	10 billion won
Invitation of related firms in the region	3	5	7

Table 2-11 Economic Impacts of micro packaging material
(unit:100 million won) (source: GyungGi 'PRIDE' Research Unit Report 2007)

With the technology development in packaging explained in this book, economic performance has been projected as in the table. In 2011, an additional 10 billion Korean won worth revenue increase in expected in electronics sector with 7 firms being relocated into the region.

2.3. Forecasting for CMOS Image Sensor WLP

While previous section has explored micro packaging for its expected outcomes and technology trend, this section will explore a forecasting for CMOS image sensor WLP used in cell phone packages. The U.S. demand for cell phones would reach around 300 million units, while the total world wide demand was forecasted as reaching nearly 1.2 billion units in the same year. What has been noteworthy is that cell phones have been upgraded in every aspect of their technological capability. For example, in terms of camera resolution in cell phones, 2.0 mega pixel level camera phones have shown the greatest growth trend, followed by 3.0. and 5.0 million pixel phones. VGA and 1.3 million pixel phones were located in degeneration stages in technology life cycles. In terms of market composition, 2.0 million pixel phones took almost half of the market in 2009.

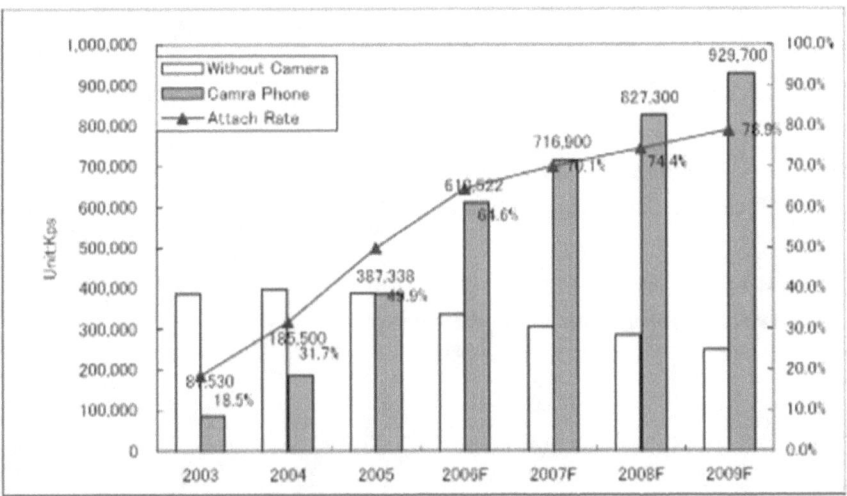

Figure 2-7 Proportion of camera equipped cell phones among total cell phones market
(source: Techno Systems Research Co., Ltd. 2006)

Figure 2-7 shows that around 78% of cell phones now on sale are camera equipped phones, which highlights increased demand for upgraded packaging requirements. It is possible to see the phenomenon of camera phone trend from a different dissection. As of 2008 and 2009 in Japan, the percentage of cell phones with camera function reached 96.8% and 97.3% respectively. Similarly, in Korea, the rate was 96% both in 2008 and 2009. The rat is a little bit low in the U.S. and Europe in 2009 with 80.2% in Europe and 78.1% in the U.S. As a total, about 78.9% of cell phones were equipped with camera function in 2009.

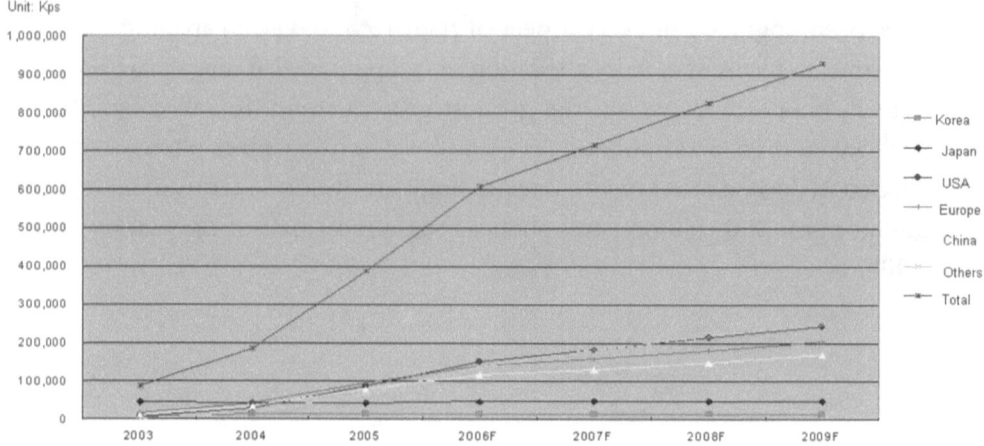

Figure 2-8 Numbers of camera equipped cell phones by country
(source: Techno Systems Research Co., Ltd. 2006)

Figures 2-8 shows the camera equipment trend world wide and a Korea-Japan comparison with graphics.

CHAPTER 3

EVALUATION ON TECHNOLOGY MARKETING

Four IT technology development cases

1. Framework of Evaluation and Survey

This chapter undertakes an evaluation of technology development projects within the scope of micro packaging and related technologies. A focus on the evaluation in this chapter is narrowly focusing on implications for technology marketing by heavily borrowing from the concept of technology marketing and technology life cycle theory.

Method of Evaluation

As for the view point of evaluation, this evaluation took four perspectives to have a balanced outlook. First, inside view evaluation means researchers who have been undertaking the projects for several years during the project contract years are given the same questions that were given to external evaluators so that this research could have an opportunity to compare the both. It would be a litmus test for the external evaluation to see whether they are objectively carried out. At the same time, it would be a fine chance to see whether inside researchers have a blinded view on their own technology projects. This comprises the first two perspectives.

Second, as for the third perspective, this research employed technology life cycle theory to evaluate relative positions of technologies. Yet, in the first two perspectives of inside and external views, this technology life cycle perspectives is melted in questionnaires. Finally, this chapter utilized BCG based analysis so that the implications for patent pool policy can be drawn.

Sub-Division of technology projects

There are four different sub-projects related to micro packaging. Yet all the four projects differed in their level of research whether it is at material level or product development, and fields of research. The first project, which is indicated as 'technology #1' comprises of micro packaging process technology development, which is converting the material into packaging products, and securing reliability in manufacturing. The second project, called in this book as 'technology # 2', focused on developing and manufacturing of micro packaging material and parts like conductive balls and flexible PCBs. 'Technology # 3' was on developing thin layer capacitor, embedding technology acquisition, and wafer level CSP and WLP, which are the core technology to camera module in phones, development. Finally, 'technology # 4' is much geared toward commercialization and application of the micro packaging technology.

2. Inside view from research development groups: *Inside view vs. Outside view: Technology Life Cycle based evaluation I*

1) Positioning on R& D stage

Evaluation was carried out to figure out relative positioning of each technology development project 1 through 4. For scoring the following criteria was used.

<Criteria for scoring>

10points: This technology has proven technological feasibility through prototype & testing, and is at market entrance stage.
8points: This technology is at prototype manufacturing stage.
6points: This technology has completed R&D.
4points: This technology is in ongoing R&D stage.
2points: This technology is in the idea development stage

| Score of tech | | | 8.0 | 7.4 | tech1(6.5) tech2(6.7) | | | | |

Technology Development and Marketing

Tech			tech3	tech4	tech1 tech2				
Scale	10	9	8	7	6	5	4	3	2	1

Table 3-1 Positioning on R& D stage

Technology 3, which is related to camera module and thin layer capacitator development, scored the highest, which means that the technology has proven technological feasibility through prototype & testing, and is at market entrance stage. After this, technology # 4, commercialization of micro packaging technology, took the next position, which shows the technology is near market entrance. Other two, technology # 1 and 2 also showed that their development stage in completed, since the scores were all over 6. Thus, it would b fair to conclude that technology development goals for the four projects are fulfilled.

2) Degrees of innovativeness in technology development project

In terms of degrees of innovativeness, the four micro packaging technology development projects were evaluated, in which technology # 3 achieved, from the inside view, the highest scores. This shows that the development of camera

---
<Criteria for scoring>

10points: This technology is an innovative development.
8points: This technology is a major breakthrough from the existing ones.
4points: This technology is a limited change variant of the existing ones, which has almost no differentication vis-à-vis the existing ones.
2points: This technology is a minimal change variant from the existing ones.

---

module and thin layer capcitator development showed innovative nature among the four projects, followed by technology # 2, which is developing micro packaging material and parts. Technology # 4, which was geared toward commercialization of micro packaging technology marked the lowest reflecting the nature of technology development.

Score of tech	10		8	tech1(7.8) tech4(7.7)						
Tech	Tech3		Tech2	Tech1 Tech4						
Scale	10	9	8	7	6	5	4	3	2	1

Table 3-2 Degrees of innovativeness in technology development project

3) Diagnosis of technology: congruence with the technology trend in relevant technology clusters

One of the technology evaluation items included a diagnosis of whether the technology development is congruent with the technology development trend in relevant technology clusters.

<Criteria for scoring>

10points: This technology is the leading edge technology and coincides with the directions of technology development in the relevant technology clusters.

8points: This technology coincides with the directions of technology development in the relevant technology clusters, yet this one has limitations to be called as the leading technology due to the existence of competitive rival or similar technologies or technology.

6points: This technology coincides with the directions of technology development in the relevant technology clusters, yet this one is not a new technology and there are competing ones.

4points: This technology development is against the direction of technology development in the relevant technology clusters, yet there are some possible applications from this one.

2points: This technology development is completely against the technology development trend in relevant technology clusters, and it is not feasible to expect applications.

Score of tech	10	tech1(9) tech4(9)	8.3							

Tech	Tech3	Tech1 Tech4	Tech2						
Scale	10	9	8	7	6	5	4	3	2	1

Table 3-3 **Diagnosis of technology: congruence with the technology trend in relevant technology clusters**

On this criteria, technology # 3 marked the highest, followed by technology # 4 and 1 with the equal scores. Regarding the interpretation, camera module and thin layer development were regarded as the leading edge technology and coincide with the directions of technology development in the relevant technology clusters. In comparison, technology # 2 numbered the lowest, which signifies, based on the researchers' viewpoint, that the theme of the technology project 2, developing micro packaging material and parts, coincides with the directions of technology development in the relevant technology clusters, yet this one has limitations to be called as the leading technology due to the existence of competitive rival or similar technologies or technology.

Although there is a ranking among the four technology projects, it clearly shows a relative positioning. The lowest marked technology # 2 still recorded score of 8 on the 10 point scale.

4) Relative positioning on technology life cycle curve

> <Criteria for scoring>
>
> 10points: In terms of technology life cycle, this technology is located at introduction or growth stage, which gurantees application of this technology for a comparatively long time.
> 8points: In terms of technology life cycle, this technology is located at introduction or growth stage, and the range of application is being inceased.
> 6points: In terms of technology life cycle, this technology is located at maturity or degeneration stage, yet there is a range of application to be exploited.
> 4points: In terms of technology life cycle, this technology is located at introduction or growth stage, yet there should be some verification regarding application of the technology.
> 2points: In terms of technology life cycle, this technology is located at degeneration stage, in which technological change is very limited and application is limited to a narrow band.

This evaluation asked inside researchers about their evaluation of each technology projects on technology life cycles, in which higher marks imply that there is a long technology life time left for that this technology. For this evaluation measure, technology 4, which is on commercialization of micro packaging technology, recorded the highest scores.

Score of tech	9.5	Tech3(9)	Tech1(8.7) Tech2(8)						
Tech	Tech 4	Tech3	Tech1 Tech2						
Scale	10	9	8	7	6	5	4	3	2	1

Table 3-4 Relative positioning on technology life cycle curve

In comparison, technology 3 marked the second highest, followed by technology 1 and 2. It was a fresh and different result vis-à-vis the results from other evaluation items with an implication that commercialization of micro packaging has much market potentials left over. Technology 2, developing micro packaging material and parts, marked the lowest against an expectation that this part of technology development would have the longest market potentials. Developing camera module and related technology, the technology # 3, had the second highest seat, which shows that this application also has a relatively long technology life. This can be understood, in some sense, that there are numerous electronic applications using camera functions in the market.

5) Easiness to protect patent rights of technology under development

<Criteria for scoring>

10points: For patents, it is possible to state the request items, including the core contents of technology, very clearly.
8points: For patents, it is possible to state the request items, including the core contents of technology, relatively clearly.
6points: For patents, it is possible to state the request items, including the core contents of technology. Yet, it is not clearly represented.
4points: The core contents of technology can only be partially stated, which implies that evasive design to avoid patent protection is possible and the use of alternative technology can not be discouraged.
2points: The core contents of technology can not be protected appropriately.

Score of tech	10			Tech1(7.5) Tech2(7.3) Tech4(7)						
Tech	Tech 3			Tech1 Tech2 Tech4						
Scale	10	9	8	7	6	5	4	3	2	1

Table 3-5 Easiness to protect patent rights of technology under development

The evaluation in this research also asked on the easiness of protecting patent rights of technology under development. Answers to this evaluation item also gave another reshuffling of previous answers, yet the answers were quite reasonable from a technology policy point of view.

Technology #3, developing camera modules and related technology, very naturally marked the highest, which implies that this type of technology can be relatively easily patented and armed with legal protection. Also it is possible to infer that camera module related technology can easily be 're-packaged' into a new set of technologies, which makes it easier to add new royalty related claims. In contrast, technology #2, which is to develop micro packaging material and parts, and technology # 4, which is related to commercialization of micro packaging technology, recorded relatively lower marks, which clearly reflects that, these types of technologies are hard to protect.

Arguably, whether material and parts technology are harder to protect or not remains as a topic to delve into. In some sense, the total benefits from a material patent may be much heftier than a conventional patent from a module. Yet, if one scrutinizes pure easiness of filing and protecting whether the technology rights are breached or not, responses to this evaluation item is something that can easily be understood.

6) Application to markets

> <Criteria for scoring>
>
> 10points: Related technologies are commercialized worldwide.
> 8points: Related technologies are commercialized partially domestically or in the world market.
> 6points: Related technologies are expected to be commercialized in a few years based on market forecast.
> 4points: Related technologies are expected to be commercialized in the long term, based on market forecast.
> 2points: Related technologies have no commercialization cases or there has been low possibility of success even in the case of commercialization efforts. This trend will prevail in the future.

Score of tech			Tech3(8) Tech2(8) Tech4(8)		6.5					
Tech			Tech3 Tech2 Tech4		Tech 1					
Scale	10	9	8	7	6	5	4	3	2	1

Table 3-6 Application to markets

Another evaluation item was on application in the markets, on which higher marks are given to a technology when related technologies are commercialized worldwide. In contrast, when related technologies have no commercialization cases or there has been low possibility of success even in the case of commercialization efforts and if the trend is likely to prevail in the future, the lowest scores were given.

On this item, except for technology # 1, all other three technology items were clustered on the score of 8, which shows that related technologies are commercialized partially domestically or in the world market. Technology # 1, comprised of micro packaging process technology development to convert the material into packaging products, and securing reliability in manufacturing, marked the lowest.

7) Existence of potential markets and the coverage of Industrial linkages

<Criteria for scoring>

10points: For the technology, there are multiple markets and products where the technology can be applied.
8points: There is a single market for the technology, yet there may be multiple products where the technology can be applied.
6points: There is a single market for the technology, and there is a single product where the technology can be applied.
4points: Currently, there is no market for the technology, yet it is feasible in the future.
2points: There was a market in the past, yet it is expected to be perished in the near future.

Score of tech		9	Tech3(8.5) Tech2(8.2) Tech4(8.2)							
Tech		Tech1	Tech3 Tech2 Tech4							
Scale	10	9	8	7	6	5	4	3	2	1

Table 3-7 Existence of potential markets and the coverage of Industrial linkages

For technology policy pint of view as well as industry practitioners' point of view, the existence of potential markets and industrial linkages is a salient issue. To meet this evaluation purpose, this evaluation took this item. On this item, technology # 1, which is micro packaging process technology development, got the highest scores, followed by technology # 3, which is camera module and related technology. After those, technology # 4 and 2 got the same score. Even though there is a scale and spectrum among the four technology projects, all the four technologies marked over score of 8, which means that there is a single market for the technology, yet there may be multiple products where the technology can be applied.

8) Positioning of Related markets and industries on Technology life Cycles

<Criteria for scoring>

10points: This technology is in growth stage.
8points: This technology is in transition from introduction to growth stage.
6points: This technology in transition from growth to maturity stage or in the maturity stage.
4points: This technology is in transition from maturity to degeneration stage.
2points: This technology is in degeneration stage.

Score of tech		Tech3(9) Tech4(9)	Tech2(8.8)	7.5					
Tech		Tech3 Tech4	Tech2	Tech1					
Scale	10	9	8	7	6	5	4	3	2	1

Table 3-8 Positioning of Related markets and industries on Technology life Cycles

On this criteria, technology, technology # 1, the development of micro packaging process to convert the material into packaging products, and securing reliability in manufacturing, showed the lowest positioning, which means that this type of technology is in transition from growth to maturity stage or in the maturity stage.

Except for this technology # 1, all other three technology projects marked either 9 or close to 9 points, which strongly suggests that these technology are in growth stage.

9) Magnitude of market demands for patented technology of the field

<Critieria for scoring>

10points: There is very large demand for patented technology.
8points: There is large demand for patented technology.
6points: There is some demand for patented technology.
4points: There is limited demand for patented technology.
2points: There is very limited demand for patented technology.

Score of tech	10		8	Tech1(7.8) Tech2(7.5)						
Tech	Tech3		Tech 4	Tech1 Tech2						
Scale	10	9	8	7	6	5	4	3	2	1

Table 3-9 Magnitude of market demands for patented technology of the field

In terms of market demand, camera module and related technology marked the highest scores, which is related to technology # 3, followed by technology # 4, which is related to commercialization of micro packaging technology. For technology 3 and 4, it is possible to infer that there are either very large or large markets. Technology # 2, which is to develop micro packaging material and parts, recorded the lowest marks, which reflects the characteristics of material market, compared to products market where demand can be created.

10) Entry Barriers due to regulation policy or other institutions

<Criteria for scoring>

10points: There are legal, institutional incentives which make market entrance easier.
8points: It is possible that there would be legal and institutional incentives in the future.
6points: There is no legal and institutional incentives or barriers to market entrance.
4points: It is possible that there would be legal and institutional barriers to market entrance in the future.
2points: There are multiple legal and institutional barriers, which make market entrance difficult.

Score of tech			8	Tech4(7.8) Tech2(7.8)		Tech3(5.5)				
Tech			Tech 1	Tech4 Tech2		Tech3				
Scale	10	9	8	7	6	5	4	3	2	1

Table 3-10 Entry Barriers due to regulation policy or other institutions

Entry barriers are big hurdles to commercialization of technology development. On this evaluation item, technology # 3 marked the lowest position. Technology # 3 is camera module and related technology development. It is quite eye-catching in the sense that this type of technology definitely has great market potentials, which is evidenced by other evaluation items, yet this type of technology is clearly susceptible against non-market barriers like institutions or regulation.

In comparison, the highest marked technology project was technology # 1, which is development of micro packaging process. Technology # 4, commercialization project, and technology # 2, which is material development, recorded relatively high scores, meaning that they are relatively free from possible barriers. Technology # 1 even can expect some promotional incentives based on evaluation point of view.

3. Outside view: Evaluation from Micro-Joining Association

1) Positioning on R& D stage

> <Criteria for scoring>
>
> 10points: This technology has proven technological feasibility through prototype & testing, and is at market entrance stage.
> 8points: This technology is at prototype manufacturing stage.
> 6points: This technology has completed R&D.
> 4points: This technology is in ongoing R&D stage.
> 2points: This technology is in the idea development stage.

Score of tech				7.17	Tech1(6.54) Tech3(6.96) Tech4(6.70)				
Tech				Tech2	Tech1 Tech3 Tech 4				
Scale	10	9	8	7	6	5	4	3	2	1

Table 3-11 Outside View: Positioning on R& D stage

In contrast to the inside evaluation, outside evaluation marked technology #2, which is developing and manufacturing of micro packaging material and parts, as the highest scoring technology. This means that the higher a technology scores, the earlier that technology is located on technology life cycle. In the inside evaluation, technology # 3, which is related to camera module and thin layer capacitor development, scored the highest.

What was impressive was that the difference between the highest and lowest marked technology was reduced to a minimal difference in the outside evaluation.

2) Degrees of innovativeness in technology development project

On this criteria, all the four technologies marked very similar scores.

<Criteria for scoring>

10points: This technology is an innovative development.
8points: This technology is a major breakthrough from the existing ones.
6points: This technology is a conventional upgrade from the existing ones.
4points: This technology is a limited change variant of the existing ones, which has almost no differentication vis-à-vis the existing ones.
2points: This technology is a minimal change variant from the existing ones.

Score of tech			Tech1(8.21) Tech2(8.27) Tech3(8.33) Tech4(8.17)						
Tech			Tech1 Tech2 Tech3 Tech 4						
Scale	10	9	8	7	6	5	4	3	2	1

Table 3-12 Outside View: Degrees of innovativeness in technology development project

While in the inside evaluation technology # 3 outscored the others, in outside evaluation, all the 4 technologies showed a converging scores, which shows that the four technologies are evaluated as technologies with major breakthroughs from the existing ones.

3) Diagnosis of technology: congruence with the technology trend in relevant technology clusters

<Criteria for scoring>

10points: This technology is the leading edge technology and coincides with the directions of technology development in the relevant technology clusters.

8points: This technology coincides with the directions of technology development in the relevant technology clusters, yet this one has limitations to be called as the leading technology due to the existence of competitive rival or similar technologies or technology.
6points: This technology coincides with the directions of technology development in the relevant technology clusters, yet this one is not a new technology and there are competing ones.
4points: This technology development is against the direction of technology development in the relevant technology clusters, yet there are some possible applications from this one.
2points: This technology development is completely against the technology development trend in relevant technology clusters, and it is not feasible to expect applications.

Score of tech			Tech1(8) Tech2(8) Tech3(8.5) Tech4(8.13)							
Tech			Tech1 Tech2 Tech3 Tech 4							
Scale	10	9	8		7	6	5	4	3	2	1

Table 3-13 Outside View: Diagnosis of technology: congruence with the technology trend in relevant technology clusters

On the criteria that asks whether a technology is congruent with technology development trend in relevant technology clusters, technology # 3 showed the highest scores, yet the gap between the highest and lowest marking technology as well overall range of scores has been narrowed in outside evaluation, compared to the inside view. The average score of 8 would mean that the technology coincides with the directions of technology development in the relevant technology clusters, yet this one has limitations to be called as the leading technology due to the existence of competitive rival or similar technologies or technology.

4) Relative positioning on technology life cycle curve

<Criteria for scoring>
10points: In terms of technology life cycle, this technology is located at introduction or growth stage, which gurantees application of this technology for a comparatively long time.
8points: In terms of technology life cycle, this technology is located at introduction or growth stage, and the range of application is being inceased.
6points: In terms of technology life cycle, this technology is located at maturity or degeneration stage, yet there is a range of application to be exploited.
4points: In terms of technology life cycle, this technology is located at introduction or growth stage, yet there should be some verification regarding application of the technology.
2points: In terms of technology life cycle, this technology is located at degeneration stage, in which technological change is very limited and application is limited to a narrow band.

Score of tech				Tech1(7.68) Tech2(7.6) Tech3(7.75) Tech4(7.68)					
Tech				Tech1 Tech2 Tech3 Tech 4					
Scale	10	9	8	7	6	5	4	3	2	1

Table 3-14 Outside View: Relative positioning on technology life cycle curve

On the relative positioning on technology life cycle curve, outside evaluation gave a converging scores on the four technologies, which signifies that all four technologies are located between growth and maturity stages. In contrast, from the inside evaluation, technology # 4, commercialization and application of the micro packaging technology, was evaluated as being located in either early growth or introduction stage on technology life cycle curve, while technology # 2, which is developing and manufacturing of micro packaging material and parts, was assessed as in the growth stage. Yet, even in the inside evaluation, despite the fact that there was a spectrum, all the four technologies were located either in introduction or growth stage.

5) Easiness to protect patent rights of technology under development

<Criteria for scoring>

10points: For patents, it is possible to state the request items, including the core contents of technology, very clearly.
8points: For patents, it is possible to state the request items, including the core contents of technology, relatively clearly.
6points: For patents, it is possible to state the request items, including the core contents of technology. Yet, it is not clearly represented.
4points: The core contents of technology can only be partially stated, which implies that evasive design to avoid patent protection is possible and the use of alternative technology can not be discouraged.
2points: The core contents of technology can not be protected appropriately.

Score of tech				Tech1(7.18)	Tech2(6.97) Tech3(6.97) Tech4(6.96)					
Tech				Tech1	Tech2 Tech3 Tech 4					
Scale	10	9	8	7	6	5	4	3	2	1

Table 3-15 Outside View: Easiness to protect patent rights of technology under development

On this outside evaluation showed a remarkable divergence vis-à-vis internal reviewers. Inside evaluation, as discussed in the previous section, has revealed that technology # 3 had the highest scores, which means that technology # 3 is apt to be protected by patent system. In contrast, outside evaluation has shown that all four technologies did not present much difference in terms of easiness of protection through patent system. In pure numeric, technology # 1 has the slightest lead, yet this does not bear any significant meaning.

6) Application to markets

> <Criteria for scoring>
>
> 10points: Related technologies are commercialized worldwide.
> 8points: Related technologies are commercialized partially domestically or in the world market.
> 6points: Related technologies are expected to be commercialized in a few years based on market forecast.
> 4points: Related technologies are expected to be commercialized in the long term, based on market forecast.
> 2points: Related technologies have no commercialization cases or there has been low possibility of success even in the case of commercialization efforts. This trend will prevail in the future.

On the criteria of application to markets, both inside and outside evaluation seems to have agreed on a general tendency. In both evaluation, scores converged for most technologies. Inside views have converged on point 8 on a 10 point scale, while outside views were concentrated near a score of 7. Score of 8 means that related technologies are commercialized partially domestically or in the world market, while score of 7 means commercialization would take place in the near future. Thus, it would be fair to infer that outside evaluators saw the technologies as promising ones in the future, while inside reviewers regarded it as already materialized technologies.

Score of tech				Tech3(7.23) Tech4(7.03)	Tech1(6.79) Tech2(6.98)					
Tech				Tech3 Tech4	Tech1 Tech2					
Scale	10	9	8	7	6	5	4	3	2	1

Table 3-16 Outside View: Application to markets

7) Existence of potential markets and the coverage of Industrial linkages

<Criteria for scoring>

10points: For the technology, there are multiple markets and products where the technology can be applied.
8points: There is a single market for the technology, yet there may be multiple products where the technology can be applied.
6points: There is a single market for the technology, and there is a single product where the technology can be applied.
4points: Currently, there is no market for the technology, yet it is feasible in the future.
2points: There was a market in the past, yet it is expected to be perished in the near future.

Score of tech			Tech1(8.57) Tech2(8.21) Tech3(8.02) Tech4(8.27)							
Tech			Tech1 Tech2 Tech3 Tech4							
Scale	10	9	8	7	6	5	4	3	2	1

Table 3-17 Outside View: Existence of potential markets and the coverage of Industrial linkages

On the criteria of existence of potential markets and the coverage of industrial linkages, outside evaluation had a converging score distribution, compared to a dispersed range of scores from the highest scoring technology # 1 to the lowest scoring technology # 2 and 4. On outside evaluation, the four technology projects marked an average of 8 points, which can be understood that there is a single market for the technology, yet there may be multiple products where the technology can be applied. In inside evaluation, technology # 1 was assessed as having multiple markets and products where the technology can be applied.

8) Positioning of Related markets and industries on Technology life Cycles

<Crite ri soca for scoring>

10points: This technology is in growth stage.
8points: This technology is in transition from introduction to growth stage.
6points: This technology in transition from growth to maturity stage or in the maturity stage.
4points: This technology is in transition from maturity to degeneration stage.
2points: This technology is in degeneration stage.

Score of tech			Tech1(7.07) Tech3(7.05) Tech4(7.06)		Tech2(6.84)					
Tech			Tech1 Tech3 Tech4		Tech2					
Scale	10	9	8	7	6	5	4	3	2	1

Table 3-18 Outside View: Positioning of Related markets and industries on Technology life Cycles

Regarding positioning of related markets and industries on technology life cycles, external evaluation and internal evaluation had a similar result, except for an outlier. Despite the similarity, a critical difference was found in average score, on which external reviews had an average score of 7. Internal reviews had an average score of 9, which shows that inside evaluation had an idea that technologies under development was in growth stage. In contrast, external views had the notion that the technologies are rather close to maturity stage.

9) Magnitude of market demands for patented technology of the field

<Critieria for scoring>

10points: There is very large demand for patented technology.
8points: There is large demand for patented technology.
6points: There is some demand for patented technology.
4points: There is limited demand for patented technology.
2points: There is very limited demand for patented technology.

Score of tech			Tech3(8.08)		Tech1(7.89) Tech2(7.87) Tech4(7.85)					
Tech			Tech3		Tech1 Tech2 Tech4					
Scale	10	9	8	7	6	5	4	3	2	1

Table 3-19 Outside View: Magnitude of market demands for patented technology of the field

On the issue of the magnitude of market demands for patented technology, inside evaluation had a larger range of scores ranging from 10 to 7, while outside views had a narrower range ranging from 7.8 to 8. Since three out of the four technologies were given scores between 7 and 8 in inside views, both inside and outside views had a similar interpretation of the market that there is a large demand for patented technology.

3. Technology Life Cycle Analysis II: Perceived Time Gap between development group and industry leaders

As an indepth analysis of technology life cycle, this section intends to analyze time gap in months or in order between technology # 1 through 4 and technologies at advanced firms or nations.

(1) Time gap between technology under development and advanced firms or nations with the same technology

Types		6 months- 1 year	1 year- 18 months	19 months- 24 months	25 months- 36 months	36 months or longer
	Tech#1	0.0	60.0	20.0	20.0	0.0
	Tech#2	20.0	40.0	0.0	40.0	0.0
	Tech#3	100.0	0.0	0.0	0.0	0.0
	Tech#4	0.0	100.0	0.0	0.0	0.0
Total		20.0	53.3	6.7	20.0	0.0

Table 3-20 Time gap (% of responses by outside evaluators)
(Row % total is 100%)

As one would recall from chapter on the theoretical ground of time gap in technology life cycles, pivotal decisions on manufacturing process, technology development or technologies and products can be in the hands of rivals as shorts 12 to 18 months (Mansfield). A critical implication from this study was that if developing a technology and putting it into the market takes more than three years, the technology development is becoming useless or in a lesser painful word, less meaningful. In sectoral analysis, 88% of technology development decisions are known to rival entities, while 38% is known to rivals within 6 months. This short interval strengthens the argument that if technology development takes longer than 3 years, in most sectors including electronics field, it would lose competitiveness to catch up the leaders.

Interpeting the technology projects in this book, all the four projects are within the 36 months difference zone, which clearly justifies the rationale for starting development. Among the four technologies, opinions were in agreement that technology #3 has the shortest time gap expressed in the shortest distribution of responses, followed by technology #4. On this criteria, technology #2 was relatively fragile in the sense that time gap between the technology development project and advanced firms or nations was the largest.

Yet, it is fair to say that the degrees of time gap can not justify the relative importance of technology development.

(2) Design Competitiveness vis-à-vis its rivals

Types	Very advanced	advanced	similar	inferior	Much inferior
Technology#1	25.0	25.0	25.0	25.0	0.0
Technology#2	0.0	60.0	40.0	0.0	0.0
Technology#3	100.0	0.0	0.	0.0	0.0
Technology#4	0.0	50.0	25.0	25.0	0.0
Total	20.0	40.0	26.7	13.3	0.0

Table 3-21 Design competitiveness (row %)

In terms of design competitiveness, technology #3, which is developing thin layer capacitor, embedding technology acquisition, and wafer level CSP and WLP, which are the core technology to camera module in phones, had an evaluation that its design has advanced design competitiveness over its rivals. While overall all the four technologies are regarded as not inferior in design competitiveness, technology #1, which is micro packaging process technology development, which is converting the material into packaging products, and securing reliability in manufacturing, had an even distribution on the four answers on its design competitiveness.

Technology # 2 and 4 were somewhat similar in that majority of views were concentrated on either 'advanced' or 'similar' on design competitiveness, yet technology #2 had a shorter tail in distribution.

(3) Technical Performance competitiveness

	Types	Very Advanced	Advanced	similar	inferior	much inferior
*	Technology#1	0.0	80.0	20.0	0.0	0.0
*	Technology#2	0.0	40.0	60.0	0.0	0.0
*	Technology#3	50.0	50.0	0.0	0.0	0.0

*	Technology#4	25.0	75.0	0.0	0.0	0.0
Total		12.5	62.5	25.0	0.0	0.0

Table 3-22 Performance competitiveness

On the measures of technical performance, technology # 1, micro packaging process technology development, which is converting the material into packaging products, had the most favorable evaluation by getting 80% of answers for 'advanced' criteria, followed by technology #4, commercialization and application of the micro packaging technology and technology#3, developing thin layer capacitor, embedding technology acquisition, and wafer level CSP and WLP. Looking at the table 3-3, it is quite clear that all the four technologies are at least similar or superior vis-à-vis their rivals in terms of design competitiveness.

(4) Competitiveness of Brand image

Types		Very Advanced	Advanced	similar	inferior	much inferior
*	Technology#1	20.0	20.0	40.0	20.0	0.0
*	Technology#2	0.0	40.0	60.0	0.0	0.0
*	Technology#3	0.0	50.0	50.0	0.0	0.0
*	Technology#4	0.0	25.0	0.0	50.0	25.0
Total		6.3	31.3	37.5	18.8	6.3

Table 3-23 Brand Image

In contrast to performance competitiveness, brand image consists of a product or technology's competitiveness. Technology # 4, commercialization and application of the micro packaging technology, was evaluated as lacking brand image competitiveness. Other technology projects, however, were assessed as having at least similar or advanced competitiveness.

Technology Development and Marketing

(5) Pricing policy comparison

Types		Ultra high policy	High policy	Convergent policy	Low policy	Ultra Low policy
*	Technology#1	0.0	20.0	60.0	20.0	0.0
*	Technology#2	0.0	0.0	100.0	0.0	0.0
*	Technology#3	0.0	0.0	100.0	0.0	0.0
*	Technology#4	0.0	33.3	33.3	33.3	0.0
Total		0.0	13.3	73.3	13.3	0.0

Table 3-24 Pricing policy comparison

Upon finishing technology development, what types of pricing policy would be suitable for each technology project? On this survey item, most outside evaluators marked convergent policy slots for technology # 1, 2, and 3. Especially, technology # 2 and 3 showed 100% response rates for the convergent or similar pricing policy. The second project, called in this book as 'technology # 2', focused on developing and manufacturing of micro packaging material and parts like conductive balls and flexible PCBs. 'Technology # 3' was on developing thin layer capacitor, embedding technology acquisition, and wafer level CSP and WLP, which are the core technology to camera module in phones, development.

In comparison, technology # 4 showed a well dispersed distribution.

(6) Expected Customer service competitiveness

Types		Very Advanced	Advanced	similar	inferior	much inferior
*	Technology#1	20.0	20.0	60.0	0.0	0.0
*	Technology#2	0.0	40.0	40.0	20.0	0.0
*	Technology#3	0.0	50.0	50.0	0.0	0.0
*	Technology#4	33.3	33.3	0.0	33.3	0.0
Total		13.3	33.3	40.0	13.3	0.0

Table 3-25 Expected Customer service competitiveness

For expected customer service competitiness, some evaluators gave technology # 2 and 3 inferior opinion by 20% and 33% respectively. At the same time, however, evaluation gave technology # 4, commercialization and application of the micro packaging technology, 'very advanced' opinion with 33%, which resulted in a wide spectrum of views. Still, this would be viewed as unstableness in customer service competitiness.

(7) Expected Advertising competitiveness

Types		Very Advanced	Advanced	similar	inferior	much inferior
*	Technology#1	0.0	20.0	60.0	20.0	0.0
*	Technology#2	0.0	60.0	20.0	20.0	0.0
*	Technology#3	0.0	0.0	0.0	100.0	0.0
*	Technology#4	0.0	33.3	33.3	33.3	0.0
Total		0.0	33.3	33.3	33.3	0.0

Table 3-26 Expected Advertising competitiveness

Regarding expected advertising competitiveness, technology #3 showed a remarkable view of 100% response on 'inferior' competitiveness. Technology # 3 is on developing thin layer capacitor, embedding technology acquisition, and wafer level CSP and WLP, which are the core technology to camera module in phones. Technology #2, developing and manufacturing of micro packaging material and parts, had 60% of responses on 'advanced' competitiveness, while technology # 1, micro packaging process technology development, had its 60% opinion on 'similar' competitiveness. Again, technology #4 had the widest spectrum, which signals that in terms of competitiveness, it would not be stable enough.

(8) Expected distribution network competitiveness

Types	Very Advanced	Advanced	similar	inferior	much inferior
* Technology#1	0.0	40.0	40.0	20.0	0.0
* Technology#2	0.0	20.0	80.0	0.0	0.0
* Technology#3	0.0	0.0	0.0	100.0	0.0
* Technology#4	33.3	33.3	0.0	33.3	0.0
Total	6.7	26.7	40.0	26.7	0.0

Table 3-27 Expected distribution network competitiveness

On the expected distribution network competitiveness, technology #3 showed the lowest competitiveness by getting 100% responses on 'inferior', while the most stable and positive response was found in technology #2, in which 80% of responses were in the 'similar' category and 20% in 'advanced' category. Technology #4 had the longest tail in the sense that responses were scattered from the best to the worst answer categories, which can be interpreted as unstable in accepting the network as competitive.

(9) Expected profitability comparison

Types	Very Advanced	Advanced	similar	inferior	much inferior
* Technology#1	20.0	0.0	60.0	20.0	0.0
* Technology#2	0.0	0.0	100.0	0.0	0.0
* Technology#3	50.0	0.0	50.0	0.0	0.0
* Technology#4	33.3	33.3	33.3	0.0	0.0
Total	20.0	6.7	66.7	6.7	0.0

Table 3-28 Expected profitability comparison

After technology development projects are completed, it would the profitability issue to be followed by firms to commercialize them. Outside evaluators gave a very positive feedback for the all four technology development projects. From technology # 1 to 3, the most frequent responses were found in the 'similar' answer choice, while technology # 1, 3, and 4 had answers for 'very advanced' responses. Also technology #4 had a shorter tail in responses, which increases the validity of profitability confidence. Only technology # 1 had 'inferior' answer choice with 20% of respondents. Together with all these, it would be fair to argue that expected profitability of all the four development projects are seemingly promising.

Types		6months-1 year	1year-18months	19-24months	25-36months	36 months or over
*	Technology#1	0.0	60.0	20.0	20.0	0.0
	Technology#2	20.0	40.0	0.0	40.0	0.0
	Technology#3	100.ar0	0.0	0.0	0.0	0.0
	Technology#4	0.0	100.0	0.0	0.0	0.0
Total		20.0	53.3	6.7	20.0	0.0

Table 3-29 Summery of time gap

4. BCG based analysis and Implications for Technology Marketing and patents

As an indepth analysis, this section intended to link technology life cycle arguments to Boston consulting group's BCG analysis. Yet, this section is not using the BCG analysis in its original form. Rather this section is applying the original concept to serve the purpose of the section.

4.1. Market potential vs. technical completeness

	Technology#1	Technology#2	Technology#3	Technology#4
Technical completeness	7.9	7.6	9.4	8.1

Technology Development and Marketing

Market potential	7.7	8	8.2	8.3

Table 3-30 Market potential vs. technical completeness

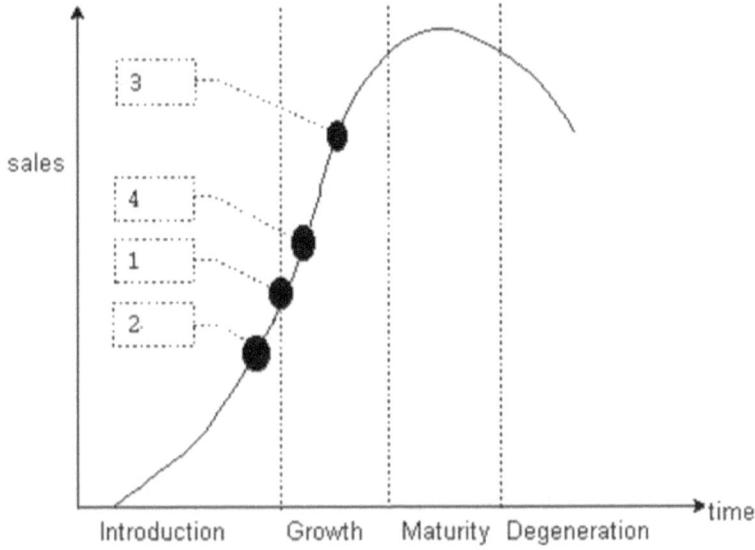

Figure 3-1 Technology side ordering from survey
(Source: Based on and re-adapted for analysis from Vernon, Raymond, 1966, International Investment and International Trade in the Product Cycle, Quarterly Journal of Economics 80, 190-207)

Evaluators of the projects we given an opportunity to asses market potentials and technical completeness of the four projects. As seen from the table 3-11, in terms of technical completeness, technology # 3 marked the highest average score, followed by technology # 4 and # 1. When one applies the scoring into technology life cycle theory based curve, it is possible to plot the four technology projects.

Likewise, market potential side scores can also be plotted on a technology life cycle curve. Then with the two criteria or dimension as two axis, it is possible to plot for the applied BCG matrix. For example, the horizontal axis refers to profitability axis. Left side denotes low profitability, while right hand side means high profitability. The vertical axis is the technicality axis. Upper part denotes high technology, while down part means low technology.

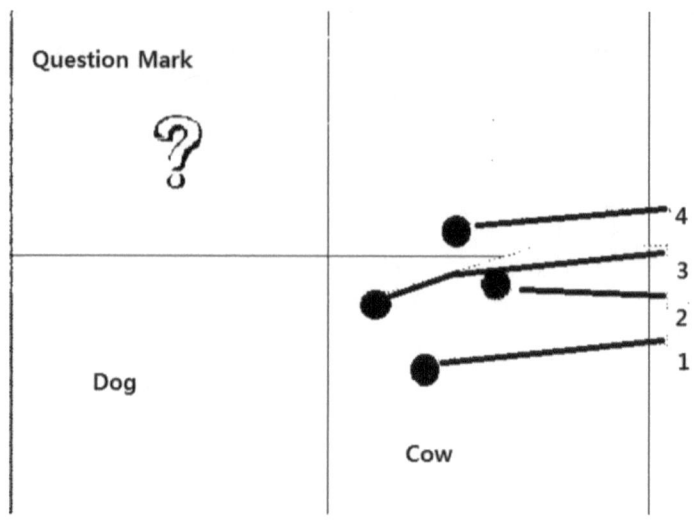

Figure 3-2 Positioning of the four types
(Source: Based on BCG matrix model and re-applied for analysis)

Based on the survey results, the following interpretations can be suggested.

When profitability and technical performance can be expressed as coordinates, all four technologies can be expressed as follows; Technology#1(7.7, 7.9), Techrnology#2(8.0, 7.6), Technology#3(8.2, 9.4),Technology#4(8.3, 8.1). It is noteworthy that all four technology projects can be considered as the 'star' projects with high expected profits and technical performance.

Among the four, especially, technology # 3 and 4 are expected to have relatively high market competitiveness, which implies that commercialization priority should be given to them would be reasonable.

CHAPTER 4

TECHNOLOGY TREND AND THE WORLD MARKET

This chapter reviews technology trend and the world market for cell phones and related technologies including semiconductors and micro packaging as a background for the discussion from preceding chapters.

1. BcN(Broadband convergence network)

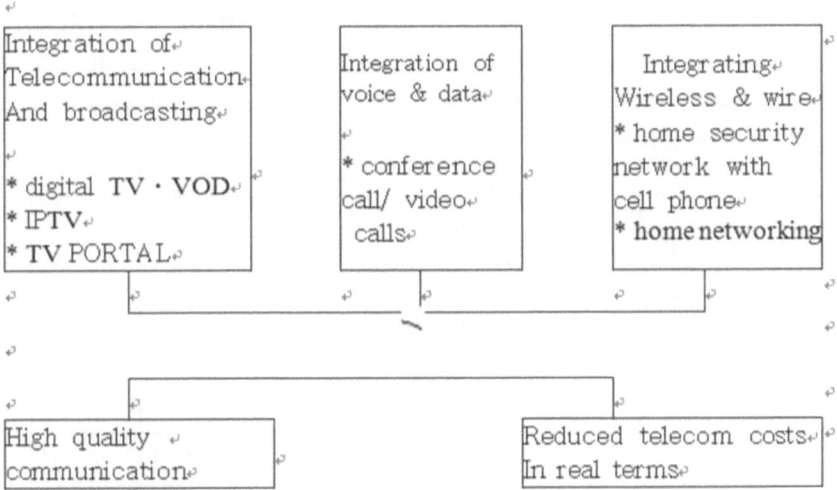

Figure 4-1 Broadband convergence network
(Source: (Source: Gyunggi Pride Research Unit Report 2007)

As for the broad background for technology projects in this book, a setting for broadband era should be mentioned first. So called the 'ubiquitous society' is what the group of technology is ensuring public as the outcome of the fast internet services. This background as the most outside environment, the next section will review cell phone technology trend and the final section will present the worldwide packaging market trend as a bridging area for the next chapter where market demand side will be explored.

As one sees from the figure 4-1 above, broadband environment 'guarantees' more service with relatively less money spent. This kind of argument hides an important point, that is there is an enormous demand for semiconductor chips, if and only if the ubiquitous society is to be attained. That, in turn, implies that there is a matching demand for micro packaging technology and related material to support the infra structure.

2. Generational division of Mobile phone market

As a final product utilizing micro packaging technology, cell phones have changed with functionalities and increased speed in different areas. As seen in table 4-1, it is possible to distinguish several generations. While the division of generations may be somewhat arbitrary, it is still useful in comparing the differences between the generations. Of course, as the newer generation of cell phones appear, need for intensive micro packaging also has been increasing.

Generation Types	1	2	2.5	3		3.5		4
	Analog	CDMA GSM	CDMA 2001 IX	CDMA 2000 IX EV-DV	WCDMA	HSDPA	HSUPA	3GLTE MBWA MOBILE Wimax EVO
Max Data speed	Not available	9.6-64 Kbps	144 Kbps	download 2.4Mbps upload 144Kbps	download 2Mbps upload 384Kbps	download 14Mbps upload 1.4Mbps	download 14Mbps upload 5.8Mbps	100Mbps
New features	Voice	Short message	photo bell sounds	High Speed Video	Slow Video call	Fast Video calls	Mobile games	High Capacity Multi Media
Period Of Commercial service	1984	1996.1	2000.10	2002.2	2003.12	2006.6	2007	2010

Table 4-1 Generational division of Mobile phone market
(Source: Korea Micro Joining Research Coop 2007)

Technology Development and Marketing

As seen from figure 4-1, worldwide users of cell phones are increasing. Asia as a total is showing that it is the greatest market. Also eye-catching is that Japanese market is regaining its market power after 2008 with increased demand. It may possibly attributable to the introduction of new services of cell phones together with new sales promotion like giving free machines for extended subscription.

In fact, service has an upper hand over manufacturing in IT world, which is evidenced in numerous writings and research pieces (Kim, J. 2008).

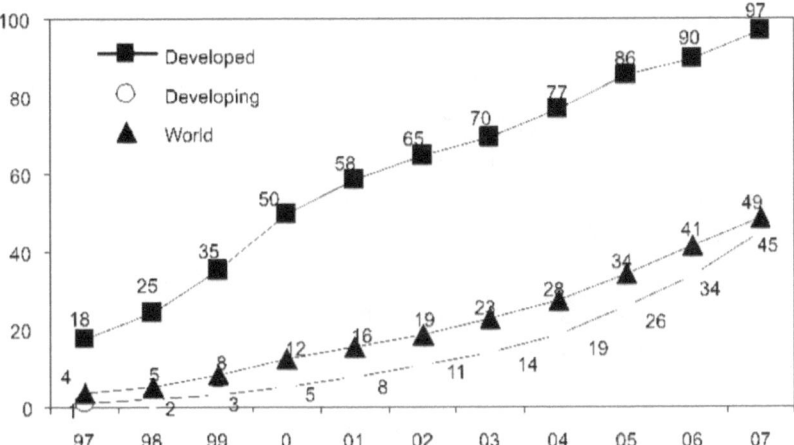

ITU statistical database 2008
Figure 4-2 Mobile phone subscribers per 100 inhabitants 1997-2007

3. Worldwide market trend for semiconductor products

As seen in table 4-3, worldwide electronics products & technology market size has been in expansion. If numbers are displayed by products, table 4-4 can show the trend.

year	2000	2001	2002	2003	2004	2005	2006	2007	2008
100 million US $	11230	9880	9850	10410	11540	12580	13210	13880	14560

Table 4-2 World electronics products & technology market size
Source: ITU statistical database 2008

(unit: million)

	cell phone	MP3	Digital camera	Notebook PC
2005	812	78	94	61
2006	897	94	103	76
2007	1156	107	109	92
2008	1225	120	111	105

Table 4-3 Forecast for major digital products
Source: ITU statistical database 2008

Going into details for discussing the size of micro packaging, it is a proxy to see the forecast for semiconductor application market. The forecast can be divided into two parts of application in million U.S. dollars and megabytes per system. Especially megabytes per system show how much chips are increased each year for the given product. The forecast, on average, shows an increase of 70 to 80% annually for the electronics product in the table 4-5, which suggests that there would be increased demand for micro packaging with the increased megabytes per system. Especially, technology development projects discussed in this book are all related to cell phone systems, which clearly increases economic viability of the projects.

Types	Application(millions)			Megabytes per system		
Types	2005	2009	Avg. growth (%)	2005	2009	Avg. growth (%)
PC	209	300	9.5	619	5184	70.1
cell phone	820	1337	13.0	45	567	88.4
Flash card	326	785	24.6	274	2542	74.5
MPC	80	145	16.0	715	4911	61.9

Table 4-4 Forecast for semiconductor application market
Source: ITU statistical database 2008

field	PC┌ server	Consumer electronics	cell phone	Industry military	Auto- motives	Wireless Communication	Sum
% proportion	39.6	20.5	19.5	8.2	6.2	6.0	100

Table 4-5 Relative proportion among products
Source: ITU statistical database 2008

In relative proportion among products, table 4-6 shows the trend. In these table and figure, it is possible to infer that the technology development with the projects in this research are closely related to automotive, wireless, and industry/ military equipment after their initial target market in cell phones.

year	2002	2003	2004	2005	2006	20	2008
Millions US.$	131	141	158	169	187	207	235

Table 4-6 Worldwide semiconductor market for automobiles
Source: ITU statistical database 2008

Automobiles today and tomorrow are more and more equipped with computer chips to meet the increasingly complicated duties that manufacturers have been requesting. This very naturally has been shown in the increased market size for chips for automobile use as shown in table 4-6.

All these demands and use in many different segments of societies ended up with increased worldwide semiconductor equipment and material market growth, as presented in table 4-7.

Types	2005	2006	2007	2008
Sum of equipment & material	638	764	813	916
Equipment	328	406	421	478
Material market	309	358	392	438

Table 4-7 Worldwide semiconductor equipment and material market growth
source: SEMI, Unit: Millions U.S. dollars
Source: ITU statistical database 2008

Worldwide semiconductor equipment and material market growth have been in a very healthy growth trend as shown in table 4-8 and figure 4-9.

4. Next generation packaging and IT

With the expected growth of micro packaging, market for semiconductor packaging equipment is growing continuously. As shown previously, cars are equipped more and more with computer based and integrated systems, which all together increases degrees and the number of micro packaging applied in the car manufacturing.

year	2006	2007	2008	2009	2010
Million US $	4930	4507	5691	4949	5348

Table 4-8 Worldwide semiconductor packaging equipment market trend
(Source: Korea Micro Joining Research Coop 2007)

CHAPTER 5

FAILURE CASES OF MARKETING: IMPLICATIONS FOR TECHNOLOGY DEVELOPMENT

Customer satisfaction & demand driven approaches have been a common sense and even a cliché in many fields of our economy & society these days. Yet, the importance of demand side can never be overemphasized. In fact, technology development is from supply side, and it is quite easy to ignore or undervalue the importance of the market and demand side. In this chapter, noting the weak point, a discussion will be presented on failure of marketing after technology development in order to glean some implications for technology development.

Like an argument saying whether an egg or a chicken is first, demand versus supply side argument in technology and product development has been in existence for a long time. What makes this argument sailient is that we find numerous decent or excellent technologies that just could not meet market demand and just fade away. Engineers and developers would hardly admit their failures. Of course, it would be natural not to admit their fallacy. Yet, their 'original sin' comes from not regarding the market, or demand side.

Rationale

Once the importance of market is understood, it would be the next step to know what would be the benefits of learning from the failures. Clearly there are advantages. Researching on product failures allows developers in the planning and implementation process to learn from the mistakes of other technologies, products and brands. In learning, the ability to identify key factors in the product development process is important. Wise strategy making can save resources and channeling them into other uses would make the developer even more competitive.

Gaining a better understanding of product failures is important to help prevent future failures. Studying the history of failures can develop some insight into the reason for those failures and create a list of factors may increase the opportunity for success. Marketing failures are not necessarily the result of substandard engineering, design or pure standard marketing efforts.

Defining product and brand failures

A technology or product is regarded a failure when its presence in the market leads to one of the followings. In this chapter, a success or failure is confined to a period or a state of technology or product after initial introduction and up to growth stage in technology life cycle, since some technologies or products later on suffer from their earlier success, which could be attributed to humongous reasons including mismanagement or competence trap.

- The withdrawal of the product from the market for any reason;
- The inability of a product to realize the required market share to sustain its presence in the market;
- The inability of a product to achieve the anticipated life cycle as defined by the organization due to any reason; or,
- The ultimate failure of a product to achieve profitability.

Product failures and the product life cycle

Most products experience some form of the product life cycle where they create that familiar—or a variant—form of the product life cycle based on time and sales volume or revenue. In some cases, product categories seem to be continuously in demand, while other products never find their niche. These products lack the recognized product life cycle curve.

Common reasons for Technology and product failures

It is possible to present some of the most common grounds for technology and product market failures which usually fall into one or more of these categories:

- High level executive push of an idea that does not fit the targeted market.
- Overestimated market size.
- Incorrectly positioned product.
- Ineffective promotion, including packaging message, which may have used misleading or confusing marketing message about the product, its features, or its use.
- Not understanding the target market segment and the branding process that would provide the most value for that segment.
- Incorrectly priced—too high and too low.
- Excessive research and/or product development costs. /
- Underestimating or not correctly understanding competitive activity or retaliatory response.
- Poor timing of distribution.
- Misleading market research that did not accurately reflect the actual consumer's behavior for the targeted segment.
- Conducted marketing research and ignored those findings.
- Key channel partners were not involved, informed, or both.
- Lower than anticipated margins.

Examples of product failures

In the below, this chapter will explore some technology and product cases where failures can lead to lesson generating. While some of the sectors were sought in drawing cases, most cases were from electronics fields, due to the focus of technology development in this book.

Automotive and transportation

In automotive fields, there are numerous examples. By naming with model names, models like Cadillac Cimarron, Pontiac Fiero, Chevrolet Corvair, Ford Edsel, The Tucker can be listed. By the standards of technology, GM's passenger diesel engine. Mazda's Wankel rotary engine, Firestone 500 tires, and Goodyear tires used on the Ford Explorer can be presented. If ones goes to a high level business strategy, it would be possible to list GM's 'world car project of 1980s' as an example of the failure case.

In aerospace, the supersonic airliner Concorde is a clear success for technology with commercially failed project.

In this section, GM's world car and the Concorde cases will be discussed.

The Concorde legend

Both French and British government signed an agreement to develop a supersonic airliner in the 1960s. Considering the time frame which is far back from the 21st century, designing a new plane, especially a supersonic one must have been a big challenge. For wings alone, it was heard that more than 300 designs were reviewed before the final selection.

The Concorde entered commercial service on 21 January 1976 with both airlines that operated it. The first Air France flight was completed between Paris and Rio de Janeiro. British Airways flew its first flight from London Heathrow to Bahrain. Both of these locations remained regularly scheduled destinations for a short time, but the vast majority of Concorde service was between London or Paris and New York City. This service was delayed until 1977 because of protests by environmental groups that opposed allowing Concorde to operate from New York's John F. Kennedy Airport.

A total of 20 Concordes were built between 1966 and 1979, and 14 of these were passenger models that entered airline service. Two prototypes were initially built, one each in France and the UK. The next two planes were pre-production prototypes used primarily for ground testing. The cost to develop and build these first four aircraft was about 134 billion and was funded entirely by the French and British governments.

The production run included 16 aircraft. The first two were initial production models that never entered service. These planes were used to test production methods and airline training techniques. The two planes also conducted airworthiness flight testing and extensive route planning operations. Five of these first six test planes were soon placed on display at museums while the remaining British initial production model was given to British Airways as a spare parts aircraft.

In 1977, British Airways and Air France purchased the first production aircraft. Five were bought by British Airways and four by Air France at an estimated cost of 3 million ($46 million) each in 1977 prices. The British and French governments built another five aircraft but could find no airlines willing to buy them. These remaining Concordes were given to the two airlines between 1979 and 1980 for the grand total of 1 French franc or respectively. The total cost of the 16 production aircraft was 54 million, but the two governments recouped only 78 million through sales to the airlines. This loss came on top of the initial development cost and had to be written off by the governments. In addition, the two governments continued to subsidize the operating costs of Concorde to the tune of tens of millions of pounds per year until 1984.

The 14 Concordes that ultimately entered service were split equally, seven each between the airlines. British Airways continued to operate its seven planes until the fleet was grounded in 2000. Air France retired one of its planes in 1982 to provide spare parts for the rest of the fleet, and another was lost in a fatal crash during takeoff from Paris in July 2000.

Following the accident, the airlines spent a huge sum of money to modify the remaining planes to meet new safety requirements before they were allowed to fly again. Air France completed these upgrades on four of its five remaining aircraft and the fifth was retired. British Airways returned five of its seven planes to service and kept the other two in storage. All production aircraft have now been retired and put on display in various museums around the world.

The GM WORLD CAR

As its grand world wide strategy, GM had its World Car project in the seventies so-called T-car, initiated in Germany. First introduced in the spring of 1973 in Brazil as the Chevrolet Chevette (2-door Sedan), it was followed in October 1978 by the 4-door Sedan, and in 1980 by a 3-door Hatchback. In October 1980 saw a 3-door Wagon, later called Chevrolet Marajó. A pick-up version was called Chevrolet Chevy 500. In Colombia and Chile there was a Chevrolet San Remo (Sedan) and in Ecuador a Chevrolet Cargo (pick-up). In Ecuador the model was called as Aymesa Cóndor (fibre glass 2-door Sedan, 2-door Coupe and pickup) and the wagon was sold as Aymesa Gacela.

In Uruguay, the Brazilian Chevette Wagon was built as Grumett 250M with a polyester body;, and was renamed Grumett. with variants like Grumett Sport 2-door coupe, and Grumett pickup in both 2-seat and 4-seat versions. In the autumn of 1974 the car was built in Argentina as Opel K-180 and the Brazilian 2-door Sedan was sold in Argentina as GMC Chevette from 1992 to 1994.

In Germany, in September 1973 it was launched as the third generation Opel Kadett (Kadett C) as a 2-door Sedan, 4-door Sedan, Coupé and 3-door Wagon, in 1975 a 3-door Hatchback (Opel Kadett City) and in 1976, a 2-door with open roof top was introduced. Opel Kadett. By 1978 the Kadett City was renamed Opel City, and in October 1977 the Opel Rallye, a high-performance version of the Coupé, entered the market.

In March 1975, the 3-door Hatchback first appeared in England as Vauxhall Chevette, in June 1976 accompanied by the 2-door Sedan and 4-door Sedan, and in October 1976 by the 3-door Wagon. In September 1976 the Bedford Chevanne appeared, a Van version of the Wagon. In the early eighties, after the introduction of the front-wheel-drive Kadett D, the Vauxhalls were sold in Germany by Opel as Chevette. In 1975 the Holden Gemini was introduced in Australia as a 4-door Sedan and a Coupé, in 1978 followed by a 3-door Wagon and Van.

In USA, the car was produced as Chevrolet Chevette as a 3-door Hatchback (different from the Kadett City) from September 1975, followed by a 5-door Hatchback with extended wheelbase by the 1978 model year. These cars ware available in Canada as Pontiac Acadian. By 1981, in USA, the cars were also sold as Pontiac T1000, renamed Pontiac 1000 by 1983.

In Japan, in November 1974, the car was introduced as Isuzu Bellett Gemini as a 4-door Sedan and a Coupé, 2 years later renamed Isuzu Gemini. By 1976 the Isuzu Gemini was sold in the USA as Opel by Isuzu,

Technology Development and Marketing

later known as Buick Opel. By 1981, in USA also, the Isuzu Gemini was sold as Isuzu I-Mark.

In Korea, Daewoo motors produced the car as Le Man aimed both at domestic and the world market. The U.S. export model was sold as Pontiac Le Man, which entered the market almost simultaneously with Hyundai's excel. In the competition, Pontiac Le Man showed inferior competitiveness.

Basically identical model was sold in about 40 different names in different countries.

Computer industry

Since the topic area for technology development in this book is in electronis field, this section will spend some attention to computer and its related technologies.

Aplple's Newton

Shown in 1993 as a MessagePad, Newton was the first PDA. It used the Newton intelligence OS with 20MHz ARM 610 processor, 640k RAM, 4MB ROM, touch screen(336 x 240), and PCMCIA, which were the high end technologies. Despite all these, its pen entry system did not work properly, and price ce was too high to generate clouds of users. Apple spent 6 years on this project not by rejecting the system.

Apple's Lisa

Announced in 1983, Lisa was the first personal PC with graphic user interface and a mouse. It used a 5MHz Motorola processor with 1MB ram. Its merit was its use of multitasking and virtual memory technology at that time. The reason why

Lisa is considered a failure in market sense comes from its price tag of 9,995 dollars, which, if converted in US. Dollars in 2007, was around 20,000 dollars.

Apple Pippin

Apple's Pippin was a multi media box comparable to Micorsoft's XBOX or Nintendo products. It was equipped with 66MHz power PC 603e processor, 14.4 kbps modem, and Mac OS. Marketing problem was that consumers were already used to SONY playstation, Sega Nintendo 64, and others, which made Pippin no footsteps to lower the entry barriers. Only 42,000 units were sold. This is a sharp contrast to Microsoft's XBOX.

Apple E-World

In 1994, Apple signed a partnership with AOL to launch the e-world to service e-mail, news and other services. The problem was from its pricing policy. It was too high to allure consumers, Together with low publicity It was closed on March 31st,1996.

Taligent

Mac aligned with IBM to develop a next generation operating software in 1988 to replace its Mac OS. Both firms made a venture capital firm, Taligent for the task. What Taligent developed was not an operating system, but a developer's platform called Commonpoint, which was transffered to IBMin 1995 and later perished in 1998.

Photographic and video

In this field, similar to preceding areas, there are numerous marketing failure cases, which include Polaroid instant home movies, X-70 (Polaroid instant camera), and video disc players. In this section, video format case between Sony's beta and VHS case will be discussed.

Beta vs. VHS

Sony's beta type videos had technological superiority over VHS type videos. Yet, 'sociology' of technology licensing made the war between the two types a failure for the technologically superior side. Sony was too harsh against the potential licensee of their beta technology to move them away to join the VHS side. Once the number of firms licensing the VHS technology clearly outnumbers the Sony 'alliance', it was the market that was affected. For example, video and movie vendors began doubting market potential for beta type movies, which may be analogous to reduced number of software available. This, in turn, gave consumers signals not to buy beta type machines.

Summary

Through this chapter, a marketing analysis was presented with different industrial segments. The rationale behind this was to 'alarm' a supply side approach to technology or product development. It is clear that technology development can not evade the born nature of supply side. Yet, not noting closely on what the market would want will ended up with fiascos in the overall success of the technology and product.

CHAPTER 6

CONCLUSION

Technology development is an important locomotive in economic development and sustanence of a society. This book, among many different topics under technology development, has focused on an micro electronics field development case with a theme of technology life cycle and market potentials. Through the chapters, a common thread to run was whether the technology projects under development have enough market potentials with theoretical and empirical surveys of experts.

To fulfill the aim set forth, this book introduced a theoretical review on technology life cycles in chapter one with detailed presentation of classic pieces and a series of more updated literature in the filed. This was to pre-equip the remaining parts with theoretical lenses so that analysis can be conducted.

An empirical research introduced in chapter one, with 100 firms in 13 industries, reported that pivotal decisions on manufacturing process, technology development or technologies and products can be in the hands of rivals as shorts 12 to 18 months (Mansfield). A critical implication from this study is that if developing a technology and putting it into the market takes more than three years, the technology development is becoming useless or in a lesser painful word, less meaningful. This was a critieria used in this book in evaluating the time between the leader and the followers in the following chapters. Perhaps the three year gap would be a critical bar.

Based on analysis with the theoretical lenses, it turned out that technology development projects under the scope of this book were found out to be relatively healthy in the sense that they still have enough technology life cycles to enjoy after the completion of the development. Also noteworthy was the time gap between the advanced groups and the followers. It was found that time gap was less than the critical level, which relieves the pressure to be concerned about commercial failure after technological success.

Technology Development and Marketing

The reason why market potential is important has been presented in chapter 5, where different commercial failures cases were explained. All the failed cases presented were technologically 'complete'. In some cases, they were superior to the existing methods or competitors. Supersonic airliner Concorde and Sony's Beta type videos would be only a fraction of an iceberg that represents technologically superior but commercially inferior cases.

Perhaps technology development side comes from the supply side, which can easily forget or have a tunnel vision on the potential sides of their development. Not because technology development side is unimportant, but because demand side is so important, technology developing entities, whether they are individuals or organizations, should focus more on market feasibility before launching the projects on a full scale.

Upon closing the book, the point that makes the development case unique was that the developers were open to market potentials from the early period, and this insight gave a feedback to their performance. Furthermore, developers introduced in the book utilized industry-academic networks appropriately, which increased potentials for successful development. As theoretical part illustrated, in today's tomorrow's research cooperation environment, a more delicate definition of cooperation scheme is a critical factor for success.

Technology evaluation is truly a subtle process and event, yet when it is used wisely, consequences of technology development are benefited more than the investment given to evaluation.

APPENDIX

Mobile cellular subscriptions (2008 ITU Statistics)

		Mobile cellular subscriptions					As % of total telephone subscribers
		(000s)		CAGR (%)	per 100 inhabitants	% Digital	
		2003	2008	2003-08	2008	###	2008
1	Afghanistan	200.0	7'898.9	108.6	29.03	...	98.7
2	Albania	1'100.0	3'141.2	23.4	99.93	100.0	90.8
3	Algeria	1'446.9	27'562.7	108.9	81.41	100.0	90.0
4	American Samoa	2.1	2.2	7.1	3.65	...	17.9
5	Andorra	51.9	64.2	4.3	76.06	...	63.2
6	Angola	350.0	6'773.4	80.9	37.59	...	98.3
7	Anguilla	8.8	13.1	21.5	95.56	...	70.3
8	Antigua & Barbuda	46.1	136.6	24.3	157.67	...	78.2
9	Argentina	7'842.2	46'508.8	42.8	116.61	...	82.8
10	Armenia	114.4	1'876.4	101.3	61.07	...	34.9
11	Aruba	70.0	127.1	12.7	120.49	...	76.8
12	Ascension	-	-	-	...	...	-
13	Australia	14'347.0	22'120.0	9.0	104.96	...	70.2
14	Austria	7'274.0	10'816.0	8.3	129.73	...	76.4
15	Azerbaijan	1'057.1	6'548.0	44.0	75.00	...	83.2
16	Bahamas	122.2	358.0	24.0	106.04	...	73.8
17	Bahrain	443.1	1'400.0	25.9	180.51	100.0	86.4
18	Bangladesh	1'365.0	44'640.0	100.9	27.90	...	97.1
19	Barbados	140.0	336.0	24.5	132.00	...	69.1
20	Belarus	1'118.0	6'960.0	58.0	71.57	...	65.5
21	Belgium	8'605.8	11'822.2	6.6	111.63	...	72.6
22	Belize	60.4	160.0	21.5	53.23	...	83.7
23	Benin	236.2	3'435.0	70.8	39.66	100.0	94.5
24	Bermuda	40.0	60.1	14.5	93.35	...	51.0

25	Bhutan	2.3	251.0	156.6	36.55	100.0	90.1
26	Bolivia	1'278.8	4'830.0	30.4	49.82	...	82.8
27	Bosnia and Herzegovina	1'074.8	3'179.0	24.2	84.26	100.0	75.5
28	Botswana	445.0	1'485.8	27.3	77.34	...	91.3
29	Brazil	46'373.3	150'641.4	26.6	78.47	...	78.5
30	British Virgin Islands	8.0	23.0	23.5	100.91	...	...
31	Brunei Darussalam	177.4	348.9	18.4	90.66	...	82.0
32	Bulgaria	3'500.9	10'633.3	24.9	140.05	100.0	82.5
33	Burkina Faso	238.1	2'553.0	60.7	16.76	...	93.0
34	Burundi	64.0	480.6	49.7	5.95	100.0	94.0
35	Cambodia	498.4	4'237.0	53.4	29.10	...	98.9
36	Cameroon	1'077.0	6'160.9	41.7	32.28	...	96.9
37	Canada	13'291.0	21'455.2	10.1	64.51	...	52.6
38	Cape Verde	53.3	277.7	39.1	55.68	100.0	79.4
39	Cayman Islands	21.0	33.8	60.6	66.84	...	...
40	Central African Rep.	40.0	154.0	30.9	3.55	...	90.2
41	Chad	65.0	1'809.0	94.5	16.58	...	97.3
42	Chile	7'268.3	14'796.6	15.3	88.05	...	80.8
43	China	269'953.0	634'000.0	18.6	47.41	100.0	59.9
44	Cocos Keeling Islands	...	...	...	...	...	...
45	Colombia	6'186.2	41'364.8	46.2	91.90	...	85.8
46	Comoros	2.0	40.0	111.5	6.20	100.0	65.9
47	Congo	330.0	1'807.0	40.5	49.98	...	97.2
48	Congo (Dem. Rep.)	1'246.2	9'262.9	49.4	14.42	...	99.6
49	Cook Islands	3.4	6.7	14.5	33.91	...	49.7
50	Costa Rica	778.3	1'886.6	19.4	41.75	...	56.8
51	Côte d'Ivoire	1'280.7	10'449.0	52.2	50.74	100.0	96.7
52	Croatia	2'537.3	5'924.0	18.5	133.95	100.0	76.2
53	Cuba	35.4	331.7	56.5	2.96	...	23.1
54	Cyprus	551.8	1'016.7	13.0	117.89	...	71.1

55	Czech Republic	9'708.7	13'780.2	7.3	133.54	...	85.8
56	D.P.R. Korea	-	-	-	-	...	-
57	Denmark	4'767.1	6'550.7	6.6	120.02	100.0	72.5
58	Djibouti	23.0	44.1	38.4	5.47	100.0	80.3
59	Dominica	23.8	89.0	39.1	132.76	...	83.6
60	Dominican Rep.	2'091.9	7'210.5	28.1	72.45	...	88.0
61	Ecuador	2'398.2	11'595.1	37.1	86.01	...	85.9
62	Egypt	5'797.5	41'272.5	48.1	50.62	100.0	77.5
63	El Salvador	1'149.8	6'950.7	43.3	113.32	...	86.6
64	Equatorial Guinea	41.5	346.0	52.8	52.49	...	90.6
65	Eritrea	-	108.6	-	2.20	100.0	72.9
66	Estonia	1'050.2	2'524.5	19.2	188.20	100.0	83.5
67	Ethiopia	51.3	3'168.3	128.1	3.93	...	77.7
68	Falkland (Malvinas) Is.	-	3.0	-	99.37	...	55.9
69	Faroe Islands	38.0	54.9	7.6	110.55	100.0	71.5
70	Fiji	109.9	600.0	40.4	71.09	...	81.3
71	Finland	4'747.1	6'830.0	7.5	128.76	100.0	80.5
72	France	41'702.0	57'972.0	6.8	93.45	...	62.4
73	French Guiana	92.0	98.0	6.5	50.29	100.0	...
74	French Polynesia	60.1	187.1	25.5	70.43	...	77.4
75	Gabon	300.0	1'300.0	34.1	89.77	100.0	97.8
76	Gambia	149.3	1'166.1	50.8	70.24	...	96.0
77	Georgia	711.2	2'599.7	38.3	59.66	100.0	82.4
78	Germany	64'800.0	107'245.0	10.6	130.37	...	67.6
79	Ghana	795.5	11'570.4	70.8	49.55	100.0	98.8
80	Gibraltar	15.9	18.4	15.7	60.48	100.0	42.0
81	Greece	8'936.2	13'799.3	9.1	123.90	...	69.8
82	Greenland	29.7	55.8	13.4	97.40	...	71.0
83	Grenada	42.3	60.0	7.3	57.97	...	67.7
84	Guadeloupe	289.4	314.7	8.7	69.75	...	...
85	Guam	79.8	98.0	22.8	59.06	...	...
86	Guatemala	2'034.8	14'948.6	49.0	109.22	...	91.2

87	Guernsey	41.5	43.8	5.5	78.54	...	49.3
88	Guinea	111.5	2'600.0	87.7	26.44	...	97.6
89	Guinea-Bissau	1.3	500.2	230.2	31.75	100.0	99.1
90	Guyana	138.0	281.4	42.8	36.84	...	71.9
91	Haiti	320.0	3'200.0	58.5	32.40	...	95.8
92	Honduras	379.4	6'210.7	74.9	84.86	...	88.3
93	Hong Kong, China	7'349.2	11'374.2	9.1	162.90	100.0	73.5
94	Hungary	7'944.6	12'224.2	9.0	122.09	...	79.8
95	Iceland	279.7	327.6	4.0	106.33	95.2	63.7
96	India	33'690.0	346'890.0	59.4	29.36	...	90.2
97	Indonesia	18'495.3	140'578.2	50.0	61.83	...	82.2
98	Iran (I.R.)	3'449.9	43'000.0	65.6	58.65	...	63.4
99	Iraq	80.0	14'021.2	263.9	47.55	...	91.1
100	Ireland	3'500.0	5'048.1	7.6	113.77	100.0	69.6
101	Israel	6'618.4	8'982.0	6.3	127.38	100.0	75.6
102	Italy	56'770.0	88'580.0	9.3	148.61	100.0	81.6
103	Jamaica	1'576.4	2'723.3	11.6	100.58	...	89.6
104	Japan	86'655.0	110'395.0	5.0	86.73	100.0	67.7
105	Jersey	81.2	83.9	3.3	95.34	100.0	...
106	Jordan	1'325.3	5'313.6	32.0	86.60	100.0	91.1
107	Kazakhstan	1'330.7	14'910.6	62.1	96.06	100.0	81.4
108	Kenya	1'590.8	16'233.8	59.1	41.88	100.0	98.5
109	Kiribati	0.5	0.8	9.3	0.79	...	15.8
110	Korea (Rep.)	33'591.8	45'607.0	6.3	94.71	100.0	68.1
111	Kosovo	...	...	...	...	...	...
112	Kuwait	1'420.0	2'773.7	18.2	97.28	100.0	83.0
113	Kyrgyzstan	138.3	2'168.3	99.0	40.56	...	81.8
114	Lao P.D.R.	112.3	1'478.4	90.5	24.27	100.0	94.0
115	Latvia	1'219.6	2'217.0	16.1	97.72	...	77.5
116	Lebanon	795.5	1'430.0	12.4	34.10	...	64.4
117	Lesotho	126.0	581.0	35.8	28.35	...	87.1
118	Liberia	47.2	732.0	73.0	19.30	...	99.6
119	Libya	127.0	4'500.0	144.0	72.95	...	70.1
120	Liechtenstein	25.0	32.0	6.4	90.58	100.0	62.1
121	Lithuania	2'102.2	5'022.6	19.0	151.24	100.0	86.5
122	Luxembourg	539.0	707.0	5.6	147.11	...	73.1

123	Macao, China	364.0	932.6	20.7	177.24	...	84.1
124	Madagascar	283.7	4'835.2	76.3	25.30	100.0	96.7
125	Malawi	135.1	1'781.0	67.5	12.00	100.0	85.7
126	Malaysia	11'124.0	27'125.0	19.5	100.41	...	86.3
127	Maldives	66.5	435.6	45.6	142.82	100.0	90.3
128	Mali	247.2	3'267.2	67.6	25.71	...	97.5
129	Malta	290.0	385.6	5.9	94.64	100.0	61.5
130	Marshall Islands	0.6	0.8	5.8	1.27	...	14.6
131	Martinique	277.8	295.4	6.3	74.61	100.0	...
132	Mauritania	351.0	2'092.0	42.9	65.07	...	96.5
133	Mauritius	462.4	1'033.3	17.4	80.74	100.0	73.9
134	Mayotte	33.2	48.1	44.9	28.40	...	...
135	Mexico	30'097.7	75'303.5	20.1	69.37	...	78.6
136	Micronesia	5.9	27.4	47.0	24.91	...	75.9
137	Moldova	475.9	2'420.0	38.4	66.60	100.0	63.6
138	Monaco	15.1	20.4	7.8	62.54	100.0	37.0
139	Mongolia	319.0	916.1	30.2	35.08	100.0	85.0
140	Montenegro	...	643.7	...	103.58	...	64.6
141	Montserrat	1.8	3.6	18.6	60.56	100.0	55.4
142	Morocco	7'359.9	22'815.7	25.4	72.19	100.0	88.4
143	Mozambique	435.8	4'405.0	58.8	19.68	...	98.3
144	Myanmar	66.5	375.8	41.4	0.76	...	27.7
145	Namibia	223.7	1'052.0	36.3	49.39	100.0	85.3
146	Nauru	1.5	...	...	...	...	...
147	Nepal	81.9	3'268.9	151.4	11.56	100.0	82.3
148	Neth. Antilles	200.0	200.0	-	108.59	...	...
149	Netherlands	13'200.0	19'927.0	8.6	120.57	100.0	73.1
150	New Caledonia	97.1	196.5	15.1	79.77	...	75.7
151	New Zealand	2'599.0	4'620.0	12.2	109.22	...	72.5
152	Nicaragua	466.7	3'038.9	45.5	53.62	...	88.1
153	Niger	82.4	1'677.0	82.7	11.40	...	93.1
154	Nigeria	3'149.5	62'988.5	82.1	41.66	100.0	98.0
155	Niue	0.6	0.6	8.3	38.46	...	38.2

156	Norfolk Islands	...	...	...	...	...	...
157	Northern Marianas	18.6	20.5	10.0	26.20	...	...
158	Norway	4'060.8	5'191.6	6.3	109.98	100.0	72.3
159	Oman	594.0	3'219.3	40.2	115.58	100.0	92.2
160	Pakistan	2'404.4	88'019.7	105.5	49.74	...	95.2
161	Palau	3.9	10.7	28.5	52.65	...	58.9
162	Palestine	480.0	1'025.9	20.9	25.53	...	74.7
163	Panama	692.4	3'804.7	40.6	111.94	...	88.5
164	Papua New Guinea	17.5	300.0	103.5	4.67	...	83.3
165	Paraguay	1'770.3	5'790.8	26.7	92.83	...	94.1
166	Peru	2'930.3	20'951.8	48.2	72.66	...	87.9
167	Philippines	22'509.6	68'101.8	24.8	75.38	100.0	94.6
168	Poland	17'401.2	41'388.8	24.2	108.54	100.0	80.0
169	Portugal	10'002.7	14'909.6	8.3	139.64	...	78.3
170	Puerto Rico	1'860.0	3'353.8	34.3	85.71	...	76.4
171	Qatar	376.5	1'683.0	34.9	131.39	...	86.5
172	Réunion	521.5	579.2	11.1	74.98	100.0	...
173	Romania	7'039.9	24'467.0	28.3	114.54	...	82.9
174	Russia	36'135.1	187'500.0	39.0	132.61	...	78.7
175	Rwanda	130.7	1'322.6	58.9	13.61	...	98.7
176	S. Tomé & Principe	4.8	49.0	59.0	30.59	100.0	79.7
177	Samoa	10.5	86.0	69.2	48.06	...	55.2
178	San Marino	16.9	17.7	0.9	56.76	...	45.4
179	Saudi Arabia	7'238.2	36'150.0	37.9	143.45	100.0	89.8
180	Senegal	782.4	5'389.1	47.1	44.13	100.0	95.8
181	Serbia	...	9'618.8	...	97.76	100.0	75.7
182	Seychelles	49.2	85.3	11.6	101.78	100.0	78.6
183	Sierra Leone	113.2	1'008.8	54.9	18.14	...	...
184	Singapore	3'577.0	6'375.5	12.3	138.15	100.0	77.4
185	Slovak Republic	3'678.8	5'520.0	8.5	102.23	...	83.4
186	Slovenia	1'739.1	2'054.9	3.4	101.97	100.0	67.1
187	Solomon Islands	1.1	10.9	79.1	2.19	...	47.9

188	Somalia	200.0	600.0	31.6	6.87	...	85.7
189	South Africa	16'860.0	45'000.0	21.7	90.60	100.0	90.3
190	Spain	37'219.8	49'681.6	5.9	111.68	...	71.1
191	Sri Lanka	1'393.4	11'082.2	51.4	55.24	100.0	76.3
192	St. Helena	-	-	-	-	...	-
193	St. Kitts and Nevis	22.0	74.0	35.4	146.78	...	78.3
194	St. Lucia	99.0	169.6	11.4	99.53	...	80.6
195	St. Pierre & Miquelon	-	...	...	...	...	...
196	St. Vincent and the Grenadines	62.9	130.1	15.6	119.23	...	85.1
197	Sudan	527.2	11'186.5	84.2	27.05	...	96.9
198	Suriname	168.5	320.0	23.8	63.33	100.0	79.7
199	Swaziland	85.0	457.0	40.0	39.13	100.0	85.0
200	Sweden	8'801.0	10'371.0	4.2	113.23	...	65.3
201	Switzerland	6'189.0	8'780.0	7.2	116.43	...	64.6
202	Syria	1'185.0	7'056.2	42.9	33.24	100.0	66.0
203	Taiwan, China	25'799.8	25'412.5	-0.3	110.31	100.0	64.0
204	Tajikistan	47.6	2'350.0	165.0	34.93	...	87.4
205	Tanzania	1'942.0	13'006.8	46.3	30.62	100.0	99.1
206	TFYR Macedonia	776.0	2'501.9	26.4	122.56	...	84.6
207	Thailand	21'828.2	79'065.8	38.0	118.04	100.0	91.8
208	Timor-Leste	20.1	78.2	40.5	7.35	100.0	97.0
209	Togo	243.6	1'547.0	44.7	23.95	...	91.7
210	Tokelau	-	-	-	-	...	-
211	Tonga	11.2	50.5	35.1	48.73	...	66.4
212	Trinidad & Tobago	336.4	1'509.8	45.6	113.67	...	83.1
213	Tunisia	1'917.5	8'569.3	34.9	84.27	...	87.4
214	Turkey	27'887.5	65'824.1	18.7	89.05	100.0	79.0
215	Turkmenistan	9.2	347.6	148.0	6.98	...	43.2
216	Turks & Caicos Is.	19.4	25.1	29.6	87.67	...	87.1
217	Tuvalu	-	1.8	-	18.28	100.0	58.1

218	Uganda	776.2	8'554.9	61.6	27.02	100.0	98.1
219	Ukraine	6'498.4	55'694.5	53.7	121.09	...	80.9
220	United Arab Emirates	2'972.3	9'357.7	25.8	208.65	...	86.1
221	United Kingdom	54'256.2	75'565.4	6.9	123.41	...	69.5
222	United States	160'637.0	270'500.0	11.0	86.79	...	62.4
223	Uruguay	497.5	3'507.8	47.8	104.73	...	78.5
224	Uzbekistan	320.8	12'650.1	108.5	46.52	...	86.8
225	Vanuatu	7.8	26.0	35.1	11.40	...	74.7
226	Vatican	...	...	...	...	...	...
227	Venezuela	7'015.1	27'083.8	31.0	96.31	...	81.1
228	Viet Nam	2'742.0	70'000.0	91.2	80.37	...	45.4
229	Virgin Islands (US)	49.3	80.3	27.6	73.19	...	52.8
230	Wallis and Futuna	-	-	-	-	...	-
231	Yemen	675.2	2'977.8	64.0	13.76	...	75.5
232	Zambia	241.0	3'539.0	71.1	28.04	...	97.5
233	Zimbabwe	363.7	1'654.7	35.4	13.28	100.0	78.1
	World	**1'417'810.7**	**4'016'062.2**	**23.2**	**59.34**	**41.0**	**75.0**

BIBLIOGRAPHY

Bibilography on Micro electronic packaging

Bajaj, Rajeev. (1995) Synthesis and analysis of new monomers for microelectronic packaging application

Boca Raton. (2005) Microelectronic packaging CRC Press.

Chung, Deborah. (1995) Materials for Electronic Packaging. Burlington : Elsevier123

Datta, Madhav. (2004) Microelectronic Packaging. London : CRC Press.

Di Giacomo, Giulio. (1997) Reliability of electronic packages and semiconductor devices New York : McGraw-Hill.

Garrou, Philip E. (1998) Multichip module technology handbook 1998 New York : McGra-Hill.

Gilleo, Ken. (2005) MEMS/MOEMS packaging : concepts, designs, metarials, and processes New York : McGraw-Hill.

Gilleo, Ken. (2002) Area array packaging handbook. New York : McGraw-Hill.

Golshan, Khosrow. (2007) Physical design essentials : an ASIC design implementation perspective. New York : Springer.

Greig, William J. (2007) Integrated circuit packaging, assembly, and interconnections New York : Springer.

Harper, Charles A. (1993) Electronic packaging, microelectronics, and interconnection dictionary. New York : McGraw-Hill.

Hollomon, James K. (1989) Surface-mount technology for PC board design Indianapolis, Ind.: Howard W. Sams. 1st ed.

Hsu, Tai-Ran. (2002) MEMS & microsystems : design and manufacture. Boston : McGraw-Hill.

Hsu, Tai-Ran. (2008) MEMS and microsystems : design, manufacture, and nanoscale engineering

Hoboken, N.J. : John Wiley. 2nd ed.

Incropera, Frank P. (1999) Liquid cooling of electronic devices by single-phase convection. New York : Wiley.

Koeneman, Paul Bryant. (1999) Viscoelastic stress analysis and fatigue life prediction of a flip-chip-on-board electronic package.

Lau, John H. (1997) Solder joint reliability of BGA, CSP, flip chip, and fine pitch SMT assemblies. New York : McGraw-Hill.

Lau, John H. (2001) Microvias : for low cost, high density interconnects. New York : McGraw-Hill.

Lau, John H. (2000) Low cost flip chip technologies : for DCA, WLCSP, and PBGA assemblies New York : McGraw-Hill.

Lau, John H. (1999) Chip scale package (CSP) : design, materials, processes, reliability, and applications New York : McGraw-Hill, c1999.

Licari, James J. (2007) Adhesives Technology for Electronic Applications: Materials, Processing, Reliability. Burlington : Elsevier.

Liu, Weifeng. (2004) IC component sockets Hoboken, N.J. : Wiley-Interscience.

Madou, Marc J. (2002) Fundamentals of microfabrication : the science of miniaturization. Boca Raton : CRC Press. 2nd ed.

Manzione, Louis T.(1990) Plastic packaging of microelectronic devices. New York : Van Nostrand Reinhold.

Madou, Marc J. (1997) Fundamentals of microfabrication. Boca Raton, Fla. : CRC Press.

Miller, Mikel Rolf. (2000) Interfacial adhesion and subcritical debonding of low-k dielectrics in flip-chip-packaged copper/low-k interconnect structures.

Ohring, Milton. (1998) Reliability and Failure of Electronic Materials and Devices.Burlington : Elsevier.

Park, OH. (2005) Lead-free solder interconnect reliability Materials: ASM International, 2005.

Puttlitz, Karl J. (2004) Handbook of Lead-Free Solder Technology for Microelectronic Applications. Hoboken : Marcel Dekker Inc.

Schwizer, J. (2005) Force sensors for microelectronic packaging applications Berlin ; London : Springer, 2005.

Schwizer, J. Force. (2005) Sensors for Microelectronic Packaging Applications. Dordrecht : Springer-Verlag Berlin and Heidelberg GmbH & Co. KG.

Soane, David S. (1989) Polymers in microelectronics : fundamentals and applications. Amsterdam ; New York : Elsevier Science Publishers.

Steinbruchel, Christoph. (2001) Copper interconnect technology. Bellingham, WA : SPIE Optical Engineering Press.

Tummala, Rao R. (2008) Introduction to system-on-package (SOP) : miniaturization of the entire system New York : McGraw-Hill.

Ulrich, Richard K., William D. Brown. Eds.(2006) Advanced electronic packaging. Hoboken, NJ : Wiley-Interscience/IEEE ; [Chichester : John Wiley distributor] 2nd ed.

Yeh, L.-T. (Lian-Tuu) (2002) Thermal management of microelectronic equipment : heat transfer theory, analysis methods, and design practices New York : ASME Press.

ASM International Electronic Materials and Processing Congress (2nd : 1989 : Philadelphia, Pa.)

Metals Park, Ohio : ASM International, c1989.

Copper interconnects, new contact metallurgies, structures, and low-k interlevel dielectrics : proceedings of the international symposium 2003

Electronic and photonic packaging, Integration and packaging of micro/nano/electronic systems--2005 : presented at 2005 ASME International Mechanical Engineering Congress and Exposition : November 5-11, 2005, Orlando, Florida, USA

Electronic and photonics packaging : multi-scale electrical and mechanical systems : 2006 : presented at 2006 ASME International Mechanical Engineering Congress and Exposition, November 5-10, 2006, Chicago, Illinois, USA

Electronic and photonics packaging, electrical systems design and photonics, and nanotechnology--[2004]: presented at 2004 ASME International Mechanical Engineering Congress and Exposition : November 13-19, 2004, Anaheim, California, USA

Electronic and photonic packaging, electrical systems and photonic design, and nanotechnology--2003 : presented at the 2003 ASME International Mechanical Engineering Congress : November 15-21, 2003, Washington, D.C.

Functional integration of opto-electro-mechanical devices and systems II : 23-24 January 2002, San Jose, USA 2002 Bellingham, Wash., USA : SPIE.

Functional integration of opto-electro-mechanical devices and systems : 24-25 January 2001, San Jose, USA 2001 Bellingham, Wash., USA : SPIE.
IEEE Multi-Chip Module Conference (Serial)
Los Alamitos, Calif. : IEEE Computer Society Press, 1992-1997.
4th IEEE International Conference on Polymers and Adhesives in Microelectronics and Photonics : 12-15, September, 2004, Portland, OR
International IEEE Conference on Polymers and Adhesives in Microelectronics and Photonics (5th : 2005 : Wrocław, Poland)
International IEEE Conference on Polymers and Adhesives in Microelectronics and Photonics (4th : 2004 : Portland, Or.) Piscataway, N.J. : IEEE, c2004.
International Symposium on Copper Interconnects, New Contact Metallurgies/Structures, and Low-k Interlevel Dielectrics (2002 : Salt Lake City, Utah) Pennington, N.J. : Electrochemical Society, c2003.
International Conference on Multichip Modules, April 2-4, 1997, The Adam's Mark Hotel, Denver, Colorado
International Conference and Exhibition on Multichip Modules (6th : 1997 : Denver, Colo.)
[New York, N.Y.] : Institute of Electrical and Electronics Engineers ; Reston, Va. : IMAPS, c1997.
International Conference on Multichip Modules : April 17-19, 1996, the Marriott Tech Center, Denver, Colorado
International Conference and Exhibition on Multichip Modules (5th : 1996 : Denver, Colo.)
Microelectronic packaging and laser processing : 25-26 June, 1997, Singapore
1997 Bellingham, Washington : SPIE, c1997.
Manufacturing processes and materials challenges in microelectronic packaging : presented at the winter annual meeting of the american society of mechanical engineers, atlanta, georgia, december 1-6,
1991 American Society of Mechanical Engineers. Winter Meeting.
MEMS/MOEMS : advances in photonic communications, sensing, metrology, packaging and assembly : 28-29 October 2002, Brugge, Belgium.

Microelectronic packaging technology : materials and processes : proceedings of the 2nd ASM International Electronic Materials and Processing Congress, Philadelphia, Pennsylvania, USA, 24-28 April 1989

Microelectronics technology : polymers for advanced imaging and packaging : developed from a symposium. Washington, DC : American Chemical Society, 1995.

Optoelectronic interconnects and packaging IV : 12-14 February, 1997, San Jose, California

Optoelectronic packaging : 1-2 February, 1996, San Jose, California

Bellingham, Wash., USA : SPIE, c1996.

Photon processing in microelectronics and photonics IV : 24-27 January, 2005, San Jose, California, USA 2005 Bellingham, Wash. : SPIE, c2005.

Photonics packaging and integration VI : 25-26 January, 2006, San Jose, California, USA

2006 Bellingham, Wash. : SPIE.

Polytronic 2005 : 5th International Conference on Polymers and Adhesives in Microelectronics and Photonics : October 23-24, 2005, Hotel Mercure Panorama, Wrocław, Poland : proceedings

Photonics packaging and integration V : 27 January, 2005, San Jose, California, USA

2005Bellingham, Wash. : SPIE.

Photonics packaging and integration IV : 29 January 2004, San Jose, California, USA

2004 Bellingham, Wash., USA : SPIE.

Photonics packaging and integration III : 28-30 January, 2003, San Jose, California, USA

2003 Bellingham, Wash., USA : SPIE.

Reliability, packaging, testing, and characterization of MEMS/MOEMS V : 25-26 January, 2006, San Jose, California, USA Bellingham, Wash. : SPIE.

Bibliography on technology life cycles

Adubifa, Akin. (2000) 'Technology Policy in National development: Comparative study of the Automobile Industry in Nigeria and Brazil', *Journal of Asian and African Studies*, Vol. 35, I 4.

Alston, J., Norton, G. and Pardey, P. (1995). *Science Under Scarcity*, Cornell University Press, Ithica.

Anderson, Philip.(1997) 'Organizational Linkages: Understanding the Productivity Paradox',*Administrative Science Quarterly*, Sept.v42 n3 p595(3)

Ammi Chantal. (2007) Global Consumer Behavior London : ISTE, 2007.

Bain, Joe. (1956). *Barriers to New Competition*: Their Character and Consequences in Manufacturing Industries, Cambridge MA: Harvard University Press.

Bainey, Kenneth. (2004) Integrated IT Project Management : A Model-Centric Approach. Norwood : Artech House.

Baldwin, R. E. A. Venables eds.: *Market Integration, Regionalism and the Global Economy* Cambridge Univ Press, 1999.

Banks, Erik (1998) 'The prosumer and the productivity paradox', *Social Policy*, Summer 1998 v28 n4 p10(5)

Bansal, Sam. (2009) Technology Scorecards : Aligning IT Investments with Business Performance. Hoboken : John Wiley & Sons, Inc.

Bernstein, J. and Nadiri, I. (1988) 'Inter industry spillovers, rates of return, and production in high-tech industries', *American Economic Review*, Vol. 78, pp. 429.434.

Bernstein, J. and Nadiri, I. (1991) 'Product demand, cost of production, spillovers, and the social rate of return to R&D', *NBER Working Paper Series*, Working Paper No. 3625.

Brezis, Elise S. (1993) Technology and the life cycle of cities. Cambridge, MA. : National Bureau of Economic Research.

Butje, Mark. (2005) Product Marketing for Technology Companies. Burlington : Elsevier, 2005.

Cameron, G. (1995) 'Innovation, spillovers, and growth: evidence from a panel of UK manufacturing industries', *Royal Economic Soc. Conf.*, Nuffield College, Oxford.

Cameron, G. (1996) 'Innovation and economic growth', *Discussion Paper* No. 277 of the Centre for Economic Performance, London School of Economics and Political Science

Cannon, David L. (2008) CISA : Certified Information Systems Auditor Study Guide. Hoboken : John Wiley & Sons, Inc., 2008. 2nd ed.

Center for Building Technology. Building Economics and Regulatory Technology Division. (1978)

Life-cycle costing : a guide for selecting energy conservation projects for public buildings

Charvat, Jason. (2002) Project Management Nation : Tools, Techniques, and Goals for the New and Practicing IT Project Manager. New York : John Wiley & Sons, Inc., 2002.

Chou, Yon-Chun., and Chuan-Shun Wu. (2002) 'Economic Analysis and Optimization of Tool Portfolio in Semiconductor Manufacturing', *IEEE Transactions on Semiconductor Manufacturing*, Vol. 15, i.4.

Clark, James. (2007) Handbook of Green Chemistry and Technology. Oxford : John Wiley & Sons, Ltd.,

David, P. (1992) 'Analyzing the economic payoffs from basic research', *Economic Innovations and New Technology*, pp.73.90.

Dasgupta, P. and David, P. (1994) 'Toward a new economics of science', *Research Policy*, Vol. 23, pp.487.521

Defense Acquisition University. (2009) Integrated defense acquisition, technology, & logistics life cycle management framework. Fort Belvoir, Va. :; Washington, D.C.

Delmestri, Giuseppe. (1997) 'Convergent Organizational Responses to Globalization in the Italian and German machine-building industries', *International Studies of Management & Organization*, Vol. 27, n.3.

DeLuccia, James J., (2008) IT compliance and controls : best practices for implementation

Hoboken, N.J. : John Wiley & Sons.

Dewulf, Jo. (2006) Renewables-Based Technology : Sustainability Assessment. Chichester : John Wiley & Sons, Ltd., 2006.

Ellingham, Ian. (2006) New generation whole-life costing : property and construction decision-making under uncertainty. London ; New York : Taylor & Francis.

Evans, Peter, et. Al. editors (1982). *High Technology and Third World Industrialization: Brazilian Computer Policy in Comparative Perspective* Berkeley: International and Area Studies Publications.

Farok, Contractor J. (1983). "Technology Importation Policies in Developing Countries: Some Implications of Recent Theoretical and Empirical Evidence," *Journal of Developing Areas*, Vol 117.

Franke, R. H.(1987) "Technological Revolution and Productive Decline: Computer Introduction in the Financial Industry," *Technological Forecasting and Social Change* (31), pp. 143-154.

Garnsey, Elizabeth and Christian Longhi. (2004). 'High technology locations and globalization: converse paths, common processes' *International Journal of Technology Management* (IJTM), Vol. 28, No. 3/4/5/6

General Accounting Office. (1988) Space station: NASA efforts to establish a design-to-life-cycle cost process : report to the chairman, Committee on Science, Space, and Technology, House of Representatives United States.Washington, D.C.

Gibson, David.(2004) editor. *Learning and Knowledge for the Network Society*, Purdue University Press.

Griliches, Z. (1980) 'R&D and the productivity slowdown', *The American Economic Review*, Vol. 70, No. 2, pp.343.348.

Grossman, Gene M.(1989) Quality ladders and product cycles. Cambridge, MA : National Bureau of Economic Research.

Guinnane, Timothy W., William A. Sundstrom, and Warren Whatley. Eds. (2004) History matters : essays on economic growth, technology, and demographic change. Stanford, Calif. : Stanford University Press

Hanssen, Ole Jørgen., Fredrikstad ; Trondheim : Stiftelsen Østfoldforskning. (1997)

Sustainable industrial product systems : integration of life cycle assessment in product development and optimisation of product systems

Hawk, Hugh.(2003) Bridge life-cycle cost analysis. Washington, D.C. : Transportation Research Board, National Research Council, 2003.

Hedges, James R. (2005) Hedges on hedge funds : how to successfully analyze and select an investment Hoboken, N.J. : Wiley.

Horrigan, John and Wilson, Robert H. (2002) 'Telecommunications technologies and urban development: Strategies in U.S. cities',

International Journal of Technology, Policy, and Management(IJTPM) Vol. 2. no. 3.

Huijbregts, Mark. (2009) Biofuels for Road Transport. Dordrecht : Springer, 2009.

Imed Boughzala. (2006) Trends in Enterprise Knowledge Management. London : ISTE, 2006

Industrial risk management: a life-cycle engineering approach : a selection of papers presented at the International Conference on Industrial Risk Management at the Swiss Federal Institute of Technology, Zürich, Switzerland, 16-17 January 1989

Jenny C. McCune. (1998) 'The productivity paradox: do computers boost corporate productivity?',. *Management Review*, March 1998 v87 n3 p38(3)

James McSheehy. (2001) 'Government R&D expenditures do not spur economic growth', *Electronic Engineering Times*, July 16

Kelly, Terrence K. (2004) A Review of Reports on Selected Large Federal Science Facilities : Management and Life-Cycle Issues. Santa Monica : RAND, 2004.

Kesner, Richard M. (2003) Hands-On Project Office: Guaranteeing ROI and On-Time. London : Auerbach Publications.

Killing, J. Peter. (1980) "Technology Acquisition: License Agreement or Joint Venture," *Columbia Journal of World Business*, Vol. 15, Fall, pp.38-46.

Kim, Junmo (2006a) 'Infra Structure of the Digital Economy' *Technological Forecasting & Social Change* Vol 73.

Kim, Junmo (2005a) "Are Industries destined toward the Productivity Paradox,?"

International Journal of Technology Management (IJTM) Vol. 29. No. 3/4. Inderscience

Kim, Junmo (2005b) *Globalization and Industrial Development*. iUniverse: New York.

Kim, Junmo (2004). 'Experiences of Technopolis in Advanced countries A section on France', in Daegu Metropolitan City, *Basic Plan for the Daegu Technopolis* (in Korean)

Lin, Carolyn A. (2006) Communication Technology and Social Change : Theory and Implications.

Hoboken : Taylor & Francis.

Loader, David. (2002) Managing Technology in the Operations Function. Burlington : Elsevier.

Logistics Management Institute. (1976) Life cycle costing guide : a guide for applying the concepts of life cycle costing to procurements by state and local governments. Washington. lst ed.

Lundquist, L. (2001) Life Cycle Engineering of Plastics : Technology, Economy and Environment. Burlington : Elsevier, 2001.

Lutowski, Rick. (2005) Software Requirements : Encapsulation, Quality, and Reuse. London : Auerbach Publications.

McCumber, John. (2004) Assessing and Managing Security Risk in IT Systems. London : Auerbach Publications.

Minshall, C.W.(1983). "An Overview of Trends in Science & High Technology Parks", *Economic and Policy Analysis Occasional Papers*, No. 37.

Moore, G. A. (1995). Inside the tornado: Marketing strategies from Silicon Valley's cutting edge. New York: HarperBusiness.

Morris, Peter. (2009) The Wiley Guide to Project Technology, Supply Chain, and Procurement Management. Hoboken : John Wiley & Sons, Inc.

Morrison, C. (1992) 'Unraveling the productivity growth slowdown in the US, Canada and Japan: the effects of subequilibrium, scale economies and markups', *Review of Economics and Statistics*, 74(3), 381-93.

Mullen, John K. (2001) 'Long-run technical change and multifactor productivity growth in US manufacturing', *Applied Economics*, Vol.33 i3.

Nadiri, I. (1993) 'Innovations and technological spillovers', *NBER Working Paper* Series, Working Paper, No. 4423.

Nelson, Richard. (1984) *High Technology Policies*: A Five Nation Comparison, Washington and London: American Enterprise Institute for Public Policy Research

Newton, Peter. (2009) Technology, Design and Process Innovation in the Built Environment. Hoboken : Taylor & Francis

OECD, (1999a). *Managing National Innovation Systems*.

OECD, (1999b). *Boosting Innovation*: The Cluster Approach.

OECD, (2001). *Innovative Clusters*: Drivers of National Innovation Systems.

OECD, *Economic Surveys* 2001-2003

O'Neill, T. J. (2003) Life cycle assessment and environmental impact of polymeric products. Shawbury, U.K. : Rapra Technology Ltd.

Pattel, P. and Soete, L. (1988) 'Evaluation of the economic effects of technology', *STI Review,* Vol. 4, pp.133.183.

Perez, C. and C. Freeman (1988) 'Structural Crises of Adjustment, Business Cycles and Investment Behavior', in Dosi et al. *Technical Change and Economic Theory*, Pinter Publishers, London.

Pinsonneault, Alain & Suzanne Rivard. (1998) 'Information technology and the nature of managerial work: from the productivity paradox to the Icarus paradox?', *MIS Quarterly*, Sept. v22 n3 p287(25)

Piore, Michael and Charles Sabel, (1984). *The Second Industrial Divide*, Basic Books, New York.

RAND. (2005) RAND Modernizing the U.S. aircraft carrier fleet : accelerating CVN 21 production versus mid-life refueling. Santa Monica, CA : RAND, 2005

Remenyi, D. (2002) Make or Break Issues in IT Management : A Guide to 21st Century Effectiveness. Burlington : Elsevier, 2002.

Renuka Mahadevan. (2002) 'Is there a real TFP growth measure for Malaysia's manufacturing industries?', *ASEAN Economic Bulletin*, August v19 i2 p178(13)

Rogers, E. M. (1995). Diffusion of innovations, Fourth edition. New York: The Free Press.

Ruegg, Rosalie T. (1980) Life-cycle costing manual for the Federal energy management programs : a guide for evaluating the cost effectiveness of energy conservation and renewable energy projects for new and existing Federally owned and leased buildings and facilities Washington, D.C. : U.S. Dept. of Commerce, National Bureau of Standards : For sale by the Supt. of Docs., U.S. G.P.O.

Sakurai, N., Ioannidis, E. and Papaconstantinou, G. (1996) 'The impact of R&D and technology diffusion on productivity growth: evidence for 10 OECD countries in 1970s and 1980s', *OECD/STI Working Paper*.

Scherer, F. (1984) 'Using linked patent and R&D data to measure inter industry technology flows', in Z. Griliches (Ed.) *R&D, Patents and Productivity*, Chicago, University of Chicago Press.

Schumpeter, Joseph (1942) *Capitaliam, Socialism, and Democracy*. New York.

Harper Torch Books.

Scott, John T. (1999). 'The Service Sector's Acquistion and Development of Information Technology', *The Journal of technology Transfer*, Vol 24. No.1.

Scherer, F. (1984) 'Using linked patent and R&D data to measure inter industry technology flows', in Z. Griliches (Ed.) *R&D, Patents and Productivity*, Chicago, University of Chicago Press.

Schumpeter, Joseph (1942) *Capitaliam, Socialism, and Democracy*. New York.

Harper Torch Books.

Scott, John T. (1999). 'The Service Sector's Acquistion and Development of Information Technology', *The Journal of technology Transfer*, Vol 24. No.1.

Sichel, Daniel E. (1999) 'Computers and aggregate economic growth: an update', *Business Economics*, April v34 i2 p18(7)

Smith, J.M. (2002) Troubled IT projects : Prevention and Turnaround. Stevenage : The Institution of Engineering and Technology.

Smith, Peter. (2005) Architecture in a Climate of Change. Burlington : Elsevier, 2005.

2nd ed.

Tavner, P.(2008) Condition Monitoring of Rotating Electrical Machines. Stevenage : The Institution of Engineering and Technology.

Turner, Simon G. (2003) Pharmaceutical Engineering Change Control, Second Edition. London : Informa Healthcare.

Vaitsos, Constantin A. (1995) Technology choice and adoption in the presence of uncertainties in productlife-cycles and technological advancements

Vernon R (1966) International investment and international trade in the product cycle. *Quarterly Journal of Economics* 80.2: 190-207

Vernon R (1979) The Product Cycle Hypothesis in a New International Environment. *Oxford Bulletin of Economics and Statistics* 41.4: 255-26

Wijangco, Mayen. (1989) "B.J Habibies: Achieving a Technology Take-Off," *World Executive's Digest*, April. pp.22-25.

Wysocki, Robert. (2004) Project Management Process Improvement. Norwood : Artech House.

Yan, Xiu-Tian. (2008) Global Design to Gain a Competitive Edge : An Holistic and Collaborative Design Approach Based on Computational Tools. Dordrecht : Springer.

INDEX

A

Aerospace 78
Apple 81, 82

B

Brazil 80, 88, 100

C

Camera 30, 37, 38, 39, 40, 41, 43, 45, 46, 48, 49, 50, 51, 61, 64, 72, 82
Cell Phone 14, 15, 16, 17, 21, 22, 23, 24, 25, 27, 28, 29, 30, 31, 32, 33, 37, 38, 39, 69, 70, 71, 72, 73
Cluster 42, 43, 52, 53, 54, 105
Computer 74, 75, 81, 98, 102, 103, 106
Consortium 9, 10

E

Electronics xv, 12, 13, 14, 16, 20, 22, 27, 32, 33, 36, 45, 60, 72, 73, 78, 84, 95, 96, 97, 98, 99, 103
Evaluation 40, 41, 43, 44, 45, 47, 48, 50, 51, 52, 53, 54, 55, 56, 57, 58, 59, 61, 62, 64, 87, 95, 105

F

Forecast 25, 27, 29, 34, 35, 36, 46, 56, 72, 73

G

Government 9, 13, 78, 79, 103, 104

I

Incentives 50, 51
Innovation 5, 8, 12, 13, 32, 101, 105

J

Japan (Japanese) 20, 37, 39, 71, 81, 90, 104

K

Korea iii, xv, 14, 16, 17, 18, 25, 27, 28, 29, 30, 32, 33, 34, 37, 39, 71, 75, 81, 89, 90

M

Marketing iii, xv, 1, 3, 4, 6, 8, 9, 10, 15, 39, 66, 75, 76, 77, 82, 83, 101, 104

P

Packaging xv, 15, 17, 18, 19, 20, 21, 22, 23, 24, 25, 26, 27, 29, 30, 31, 32, 33, 36, 37, 39, 40, 41, 42, 43, 44, 45, 46, 47, 48, 49, 50, 51, 54, 61, 62, 63, 64, 65, 69, 70, 71, 72, 73, 74, 75, 77, 95, 96, 97, 98, 99, 100
Positioning 40, 41, 44, 48, 49, 51, 54, 58, 68
Product failures 75, 76, 77

T

Technology Adoption xv, 5, 8

Technology life cycle xv, 1, 2, 3, 4, 7,
    15, 35, 37, 39, 40, 44, 48, 51, 54,
    58, 59, 60, 66, 67, 76, 84, 100
Time Gap 2, 10, 11, 59, 60, 61, 66, 85

W

World Car 78, 80

www.ingramcontent.com/pod-product-compliance
Lightning Source LLC
Chambersburg PA
CBHW030816180526
45163CB00003B/1306